Achieving the SAT® Breakthrough: Acing the Types of Questions that Most Students Find Difficult Focus On: Big & Small Ideas

SAT® Type Questions Practice Book

Published by Focus on Learning Publishing, LLC. ®

Legal Notice

Resources and Downloads:

www.folpbooks.com

This publication was written and edited by a combined team of teachers, writers, editors, and proofreaders at Focus on Learning Publishing, LLC. ® and Perfect Your Education® test prep center.

Editor in Chief: Steve Martin

Authored by: Ed Pruess, Steve Martin, Karen Jang, Jeanie Brooks

Editors: Mark Devon, Yolanda Mirez, Steffi Lau

Contributors: Jeanie Brooks, William Holt, Alina Farhan

Proofreaders: Ed Pruess, Madeline Spurs, Charlie Pak

This product was developed by Focus on Learning Publishing, LLC.®

Email: info@focusonlearningpublishing.com
Website: www.folpbooks.com

ISBN: 978-1-7330032-1-6

Table of Contents

The Abouts
About this book, the tests, and studying for the exam

About this Book & Other Books

This book is not meant to be a full test prep book with every type of question from the verbal and the math sections. This book is specifically for big & small idea questions (Also known as main idea and detail questions of a passage) which is one book of the larger Achieving The SAT® Breakthrough: Acing the Types of Questions that Most Students Find Difficult Focus On: series. We strongly suggest getting the full test prep books, download and print full SAT® tests, and then use this book and the other books in the Focus On: series of specific SAT® type questions to hone your skills on the types of questions you need to improve your score. Focus on Learning Publishing, LLC® has teamed up with Perfect Your Education® test prep center to research the data on students' tests, analyze those tests, and find common errors among the results to create the questions in this series of SAT® test-prep books.

About Practice Tests

By taking numerous SAT® practice exams, your ability to see patterns, recognize the types of questions and get an in-depth feel of the exam will increase. Taking a practice test is only the beginning. Analyzing your practice tests and finding out which questions you need to improve on will be the fundamental work. After knowing the results of your analysis, you will be able to begin the real work of tackling the most incorrectly answered questions, eventually taking another practice test to begin the whole process all over again with different question types. Depending on how much time and effort you devote to your SAT® studies, the results will show through improved scores.

About Studying for the Exam

There are many strategies, some in this book, which will help you improve your score. However, knowing the basics of the exam is important. The reading sections are comprised of literature, the humanities/social sciences, and physical sciences. The more you read texts with subjects similar to those on the reading comprehension section, the better your chances of understanding them will be. Topics found in short stories, international short stories, popular literature, research papers, textbooks (Such as slavery/abolition, women's suffrage, government, biology - human, animal, and plant- technology) and research studies are the kinds of articles you should read daily. Periodically, stories and books will be added to www.folpbooks.com for students to read. Knowing your grammar inside and out, along with sentence and paragraph structures for the writing and language section are key to success. Lastly, learning the math concepts and practicing them through the processes of focused, diffused, and chunking- learning, relaxing, reabsorbing, practicing - then, starting all over for another topic and later coming back to the previous subjects again are key study methods that will help you with the math sections, and all sections.

Your score will be determined by how much-planned effort you put into your studies, not just by taking practice tests. You need to invest at least 30 minutes for the verbal section and 30 minutes for the math section daily for about one year to get good results, more than one year for even better results. For more practice on reading comprehension questions, Focus on Learning Publishing, LLC has come out with a book specifically for improving reading comprehension subtitled: Focus On: Improving on Reading Comprehension for High School Students. As the saying goes, "Practice makes perfect." So, practice, practice, practice!

```
┌─────────────────────────────────────────┐
│  SAT® Critical Reading                    │
│  Big & Small Idea Questions Explained     │
└─────────────────────────────────────────┘
```

Big and Small Idea Type Questions

The process of answering big and small idea involves first comprehending each passage, paragraph, and sentence, then making connection, and finally applying that understanding to answer multiple choice questions. Approximately 17% of all SAT® reading comprehension questions are big idea questions, and 12% are small idea questions based on the available questions of the College Board's® 8 practice SAT® s available online. That's a total of 30% devoted to main idea questions for a passage and small ideas of a paragraph, specific lines, or sentences. Similar to the actual exam, the reading passages in this book have been chosen based on literature, the humanities, social sciences, and the physical sciences (chemistry, physics, earth science, and their subcategories) in that order starting from the 5 questions exercises.

Small Idea Questions

Small idea questions have to do with the details of a paragraph, certain lines, or specific sentences. The small idea questions deal with details that are important to understanding the passage. For example, a small idea question might ask why a character told another character the reason for doing an action in a specific paragraph, which will affect the outcome of the whole story. Although these types of questions deal with details, they are not to be confused with fact/detail questions, which will ask about what, how, or why details and their effect on something that happened in the passage. 144 big & small idea questions can be answered in this book to provide students with the practice necessary for improvement. This book, and all others in this series, should be completed multiple times for best results.

With small idea questions, you will have to understand what the paragraph, lines, and sentences mean. You should write in the margin next to the paragraph or sentence, what the question is asking about in that selection of text. Summarizing every paragraph is a good idea. You can also write what you think the selected text means. Sometimes, reversing a sentence, especially when the sentence is passive (O+V+S), unclear because of many words, or arranged to confuse you, can be helpful. When the sentence is passive, switch the subject and the object nouns and fix the verb to match the tense of the sentence. If it is unclear due to wordiness, take out adverbs, adjectives, and starter phrases to make the sentence simpler. View the examples below for better understanding:

Passive sentences:

O+V+S Sentence: The rice is eaten by me.
S+V+O Sentence: I eat the rice.
The sentence is in its passive form, O+V+S, which makes it awkward to understand, changing it to S+V+O makes it easier to comprehend and is thought of as proper writing

Unclear sentences:

Uneventfully passing each year in the countryside, the summers escaped almost as quickly as they came again, leaving us to face cruel and harsh winters in the northeast.

~~Uneventfully passing each year in the countryside~~, the summers escaped ~~almost as quickly as they came again,~~ leaving us to face ~~cruel and harsh~~ winters ~~in the northeast.~~

By removing the adjectives, adverbs, and starter phrase, we can see the basic message of the sentence which is: The summers escaped (passed) leaving us to face winters. These omissions make understanding the sentence easier for us to find the same type of sentence in the answer choices.

Shifts in a paragraph are another type of small idea question, but these are not as common as shifts in the passage explained below. A shift in a paragraph is when the writer discusses one aspect of a topic but then switches to another aspect of the same topic. Since a paragraph is usually about one specific topic, it would be odd, even confusing, to change to totally different topic unrelated to the first topic. Still, the SAT® reading comprehension paragraphs will have such shifts. Look for transitional words or phrases that change the direction of the paragraph. Words like "However", "Although", and "In contrast with" are used by writers to make a shift in the text.

Some types of small idea type questions are listed below in the categories of questions about paragraphs, questions about lines, and questions about sentences.

Questions about paragraphs:

The first paragraph serves mainly to	(Single paragraph)
What is the main idea of the first paragraph?	(Single paragraph)
During the course of the first paragraph, the narrator's focus shifts from	(Shift in single paragraph)
What function does the third paragraph (lines 20-34) serve in the passage as a whole?	(Single paragraph)
The main purpose of the fourth paragraph (lines 25-36) is to	(Single paragraph)
The eighth paragraph (lines 77-88) is primarily concerned with	(Single paragraph)
The primary function of the ninth and tenth paragraphs (lines 80-92) is to	(Two paragraphs)
The main idea of the final paragraph is that	(Single paragraph)
The last paragraph serves mainly to	(Single paragraph)

Questions about lines:

The main purpose of lines 1-10 ("Even... awaited me") is to	(Multiple lines)
The primary purpose of lines 26-28 ("the amount... labor") is to	(Multiple lines)

Questions about sentences:

The main purpose of the opening sentence of the passage is to	(Single sentence)
The last sentence of the passage mainly serves to	(Single sentence)

Big Idea Questions

Big idea questions have to do with the entire passage or a large part of the passage, for example, when the passage switches its focus to another idea. The main idea is the common idea that is shared throughout most, if not all, of the paragraphs; some mention of that idea should be in basically all of the paragraphs. As each paragraph continues, the idea will progress, evolve, and mature, and even possibly retrogress, but still, the idea in some form or another will be mentioned in the paragraphs or most of them. If the passage is written following the standard writing format, most likely the introduction and/or the conclusion will have a summary of the main idea. These are the two places you should look first to find the main idea.

Big idea questions are about the main idea of the passage, but might be worded differently, or are similar to the main idea, but asking a different aspect of the main idea of the passage. One of these different aspects could be the primary purpose. The primary purpose is similar to the main idea in that it is asking about the big idea of the whole passage, but is different because it is talking about "the purpose", which asks "What is the intent of the writer who is writing the passage?" and "What is he trying to tell the reader?" Author's purpose can be one of three things or a combination of all three. The first is to inform the reader of a topic that the writer thinks is important to tell people. The second is to persuade the reader to think in common with, or agree with, the writer's opinion on a subject. The third is to entertain the reader in whatever genre the author chooses to write the story (fiction, non-fiction, realistic fiction, science fiction, etc.). An easy to remember acronym for the author's purpose is P.I.E.; Persuade, Inform, and Entertain. Although P.I.E. might seem overly simplistic for an SAT® reading comprehension, the truth is, whether you're working on a literature passage about a woman waiting for a train, or reading a report by a researcher writing about his discovery, most writing falls under one of the P.I.E. categories. The key point to think about is "What is this trying to persuade me to think or do?", "What is this trying to inform me about?", and "How is this trying to entertain me?" For the difficult questions on the SAT®, you should go beyond the "persuade, inform, and entertain" framework to think of how the author is trying to influence the reader, you, on a deeper level.

Another type of main idea question is the central claim. The central claim is the heart of an argument presented to the reader. The claim is then backed up with evidence that supports the idea. Although the claim is an argument, something that the writer is trying to prove, it is still the "main idea" of the text.

Summarizing the passage is yet another way of asking what the main idea is. To summarize a text, you need to be able to read and search through the minor details and choose the important information and then present it as clearly and concisely as possible. As with the other form of main point questions, the key is to find the most important facts from the text, then look at the answer choices to choose the one that has those facts.

Shifts in a passage are another big idea type of question. Shifts in a passage are when the writer changes the topic of the writing somewhere in the passage. An example of this in literature would be a change in the age of a character from youth to a later point in that character's life. In science, an example would be the setting up of an experiment to the results of the experiment.

With the many different ways to word main idea questions of a passage, whether worded main idea, primary purpose, central idea or another, the key is to find the main point that the author is trying to make in the passage. To help in finding the main point, the **Passage Main Idea Web Chart** can assist you in organizing the main ideas of the paragraphs and seeing the big picture without all of the small details to throw you off the track of finding the main idea.

Some types of big idea type questions are listed below in the categories of questions about paragraphs, questions about lines, and questions about sentences.

The main purpose of the passage is to...
The central claim of the passage is that...
The passage primarily serves to...
Which choice best summarizes the passage?
One central idea of the passage is that ...
Over the course of the passage, the focus shifts from...
Throughout the course of the passage, the focus shifts from...
The focus of the passage shifts from ...

Understanding the Big and Small Ideas of a Text

Understanding the words, the sentences, and individual paragraphs to understand the whole text

Understanding the Vocabulary

Vocabulary is key. If you don't know a lot of vocabulary, now is the time to study. There are more ways than ever to memorize vocab. For learning styles and tips and tricks to learning new vocabulary, look into our book Focus On: Vocabulary. Not only will it teach you new ways to memorize vocabulary, but it will also give you practice with SAT® simulated test exercises to fortify the memorization process.

Though knowing your vocabulary is the surest way to improve on SAT® vocabulary-based questions, there are some other ways for you to figure out what a word means. Using context clues allows you to know the general meaning of a word. Look at the other words in the sentence and figure out what the word in question means. For example, in the following sentence "The deceptive liar was disliked by most of her classmates resulting from their distrust of her." If the person did not know the word "deceptive", they would most likely be able to tell from the words "liar", "disliked", and "distrust" that the word deceptive has a negative meaning. By using the words near and around the unknown word, we can somewhat figure out what the meaning of the word is, then pick the answer choice that is most similar to the one derived.

Understanding the Phrases, Expressions, Idioms, and Subject Specific Terms

After you understand the vocabulary, you need to understand the colloquial (conversational style language), literary, archaic (the language of the past), subject-specific/technical phrases, idioms, as well as lingo used in most writing. Focus On: Vocabulary also provides work on these forms of speech. By memorizing and doing exercises in these books, your understanding of elements that make up sentences will increase. This is not something that you can do overnight. To continue this work, you should read daily. The internet has nearly every article about every subject. If you focus on reading the topics on the SAT ®(literature, social sciences, humanities, and the physical sciences) along with writing down and memorizing words from these texts, you will increase your chances of improving your reading ability and subsequently your score. A list of the specific types of SAT® passages can be found at www.folpbooks.com. Months of practice and memorization come into play for memorizing and comprehending these elements of sentences, so you should give yourself at least a year of study before you take the actual SAT®.

Summer is the best time to pull up your sleeves and study for the SAT®, especially in your sophomore and junior years. If you did not achieve your desired score, plan on taking the SAT® during the summer of your junior year, or early in your senior year.

Understanding the texts - Summarize Each Paragraph

Now that we've gone back and explained the formative stages for those who need to do that work, we can get into the big and small idea explained in the Big and Small Type Questions explanation page. To understand the entire passage more clearly, it is a good idea to summarize each paragraph as you read it. Whether on or off the test, this is a good method to understand the big idea for answering the main idea type questions or the small idea for answering each paragraphs main idea and/or specific sentence questions. To do this, read the paragraph and underline the proper nouns, verbs, and things that stick out and tell you what is happening in the paragraph. Not every word should be underlined, just the main ideas. In the following example, the underlined parts indicate the main idea of the paragraph:

A young boy named James was walking down the street on a hot and humid day. As he passed by the local park, the library, the supermarket, and the school, he was in a sort of daze not really aware of anything around him. He just wanted to get home to his new religion, the worshipping of the air conditioner. Unbeknownst to him, high above the town, a menace was searching for something to claim as its own; the Dragon of Mysties' Mountain was on the prowl, and the only person on the streets was James.

Basically, the beginning of the paragraph was describing the setting and the circumstances of James. The main idea of the paragraph is that a dragon was searching for someone, and this detail is found in the last sentence of the paragraph. To better understand the paragraphs and the entire text, in the margins of the page write a short summary along the lines of: Dragon searching for someone to take, James is there. This is how you simply write the summary for an entire paragraph.

After completing the summaries of each paragraph, copy a sheet of the Passage Main Idea Web Chart to transfer all of the summaries you wrote from the margins into the bubbles so that you can get a big picture of the entire passage by looking at all of the bubbles. By doing this, you get to see the progression of ideas in the paragraphs visually, and you can more easily figure out the main idea of the entire passage. Also, by summarizing each paragraph, you are preparing to answer the small idea questions about the individual paragraphs and the sentences.

If you're having trouble with big and small idea type questions, Focus on Learning Publishing, LLC has a Kindle e-book subtitled Back to the SAT® Basics: Reading Comprehension for High School Students – Focus On: Main Idea, Details, and Summarizing with Short News Based Articles for download at www.Amazon.com or www.folpbooks.com. This book will help the students to figure out the main idea of the short news stories through writing the details, and summarizing the questions in their own words using proper paragraph structure.

In preparation for the test, during your year of study, you should definitely write paragraph summaries for each of the paragraphs in this book and any other Focus On: series. The actual SAT® is no exception. On the test, it only takes a few seconds to write basic summaries about each paragraph. Though writing the summaries might seem like a waste of time, in the long run, reading your summaries will be a lot faster than rereading entire paragraphs to find the big or small ideas. You should always use paragraph summaries on and off the test.

How to Use the Passage Main Idea Web Chart

The purpose of a web chart is to organize a lot of written information visually. Within each bubble should be written the most important information of the paragraph: the main idea. By seeing smaller chunks of information and taking out unnecessary information, the reader can focus on the main point that the writer is trying to make. Again, if you summarize the paragraphs in the margins of the texts, it will be easier to write them in the bubbles while practicing for the SAT®. However, you will not have time on the SAT® to fill in bubbles, nor will you have a chart, so get good at summarizing paragraphs in the margins and referring to them for questions before the actual test.

M.I. 1 - M.I. 10 signify the main ideas for paragraphs 1 - 10. In each bubble, you can put the main ideas of each paragraph. If there are more than ten paragraphs in the passage and you need to use more bubbles, you can draw in more bubbles to the left and right of the diagram. After you write in the main ideas in each bubble, go through each bubble and make a mental connection between each bubble, making a story in a sense. By connecting the bubbles into a story, you will be able to get a larger picture of all the bubbles which will lead you to a conclusion. The ultimate main idea of the story, the total collection of the outer bubbles, should be written in the central circle. Now, take that main idea from the central circle and check the answer choices for the question you are trying to answer. This should give you enough information to be able to provide the main idea which will match the correct answer choice for the question.

You should photocopy the Passage Main Idea Web Chart multiple times and use it on all of the passages in this book.

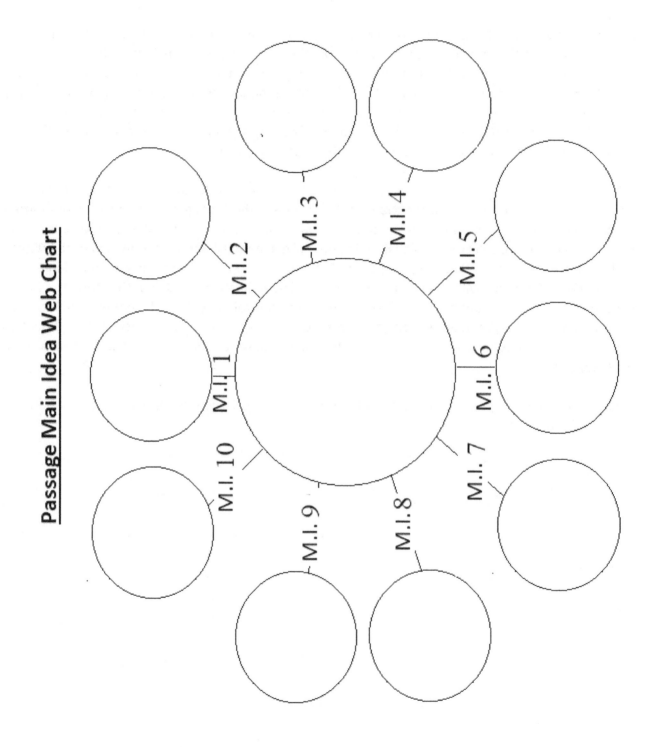

Passage Main Idea Web Chart

M.I. 1
M.I. 2
M.I. 3
M.I. 4
M.I. 5
M.I. 6
M.I. 7
M.I. 8
M.I. 9
M.I. 10

Big and Small Idea Questions Strategies in a Nutshell

1) Read the passage, then read the question. Determine if it is a big idea (main idea) or a small idea (detail of a paragraph) question.

2) As you are reading the passage, summarize the paragraphs in the margins. Don't rewrite the paragraph, just the main idea of it.

3) Answer each question in your own words, then look for the answer that matches or is similar in the answer choices.

4) Don't rely on prior knowledge; use only the information presented in the passage. Of course, knowing words and ideas that you have studied in previous texts will help you to understand what the passage is saying, but the answers to the questions can only come from what is written in the text.

For Small Idea Questions:

5) Next to the paragraph, or sentence, write what the question is asking about that selection of text. For example, "The main purpose of this paragraph, or sentence, is..." or to make it short, just write the main point.

6) For confusing sentences due to passive voice, change the sentence to its active form and for unclear sentences due to wordiness and length, take out the adjectives, adverbs, and phrases and only look at the subject, verb, and object.

7) See if there's a shift in the paragraph by locating words like: "However", "Although", "In contrast with" and see what the paragraph is saying before and after the shift words.

8) For paragraphs, look at the first and last sentence, usually the topic and concluding sentences contain the meaning of the paragraph.

For Big Idea Questions

5) Know the different wordings for big idea questions: main idea, central claim, the passage primarily serves to, best summarizes, central idea and shifts in the passage.

6) If the paragraph is structured using standard writing format, the first paragraph will be the introduction, and the final paragraph will be the conclusion. Many times the big idea will be in these two paragraphs.

7) Use the Passage Main Idea Web Chart to see what the big idea is from all of the small ideas of each paragraph.

8) Keep this in mind: What is the passage trying to do? Persuade, Inform, and Entertain (P.I.E.)? How, why, what is it trying to make you think?

The more you do this before the test, the easier it will get on the test. Do the questions in this book once, and then do them again after finishing other Focus on Learning Publishing, LLC Focus On: series book SAT® type questions. You will see that your ability on and off the test can improve greatly.

How to Use the Test Questions Analysis Sheet:

The purpose of the Test Questions Analysis Sheet is to find out and record which questions on the practice tests you answered incorrectly so that you know which types of questions you need to improve on to increase your score. Each box has a specific type of question from the exam in which you will write your incorrectly answered questions. The steps to determine what you incorrectly answered are as follows:

Take a practice test, available for free online, then check the test with its answer key to determine which questions you got wrong. In the box with that type of question on the Test Questions Analysis Sheet, write the number of the question you got wrong. When you finish the entire test, you should have the boxes filled with the numbers. The boxes with the most questions wrong in them will tell you what types of questions you need to work on to improve. Count up the amount of wrongly answered questions and write that number next to the type of question at the top of each column, or in the notes section of the page. Those numbers will tell you how many you answered incorrectly for that type of question. Based on those numbers, you can purchase whichever of Focus on Learning Publishing LLC.® Focus On: series specifically made for those types of questions. You may need to take multiple tests to gather enough data on what you got wrong. It is best to get data from at least three tests to determine which questions students got wrong. However, to jump right in to studying, one test will be enough to see which questions were answered incorrectly.

Many students incorrectly answered the big & small idea questions second most often than other questions. Based on this data, we made this Focus On: series of question-specific courses. On the following page, you will find the Test Questions Analysis Sheet.

You should copy the Test Questions Analysis Sheet and use it on all of the passages in this book.

Test Questions Analysis Sheet - Reading Section

	Detail / Fact	Inference	Word-in-Context / Vocab	Big Idea	Small idea
T-1					
T-2					
T-3					
T-4					
T-5					
	Author's Meaning / interpretation	Author's Purpose / Specific purpose	Author's / Passage Tone	Data Analysis- Graphic/chart	Line Reference
T-1					
T-2					
T-3					
T-4					
T-5					
	Function	Dual passage Comparison	Dual passage Author's POV	Notes:	
T-1					
T-2					
T-3					
T-4					
T-5					

*for a complete meaning of each type of question, go to www.folpbooks.com

The Skill of Underlining

~Basic Study Skills~

Recently, with the rise of digital distractions bombarding students' brains, more and more students are finding it hard not only to focus on the twists and turns of tricky questions, but also to read the passages themselves. The brains of Generation Z students (1995- early 2000s) have been so inundated with games, high-speed frame videos, cartoons, as well as the constant use of smartphone apps, that some neuroscientists have gone as far to say that they have developed brain disorders never before seen in humans. With these challenges, students are finding that in order to read a passage and answer difficult questions about it, they need to focus on the passages intensely, analyze the text, and transfer that understanding to the questions.

Many students are getting stuck on understanding the passages and wasting a lot of time reading them. They are not able to understand how the passages relate to the questions, and ultimately, they are failing to answer the questions correctly or neglecting to finish the questions at all. To counter this lack of focus, students are using a technique of underlining the texts that greatly help them understand the text, move quickly through the passage and retain the information necessary to answer the questions, sometimes without even having to go back and check the text for the right answer.

The Method

This method these students are implementing in their studies is called the Skill of Underlining. By underlining the entire passage, not once, but twice, then highlighting the important areas, the brain can focus on the text more than when it just freely reads. In a classroom research study, students of the class were divided into two groups, the group that used the Skill of Underlining, and the group that did not. When given a scientific passage, the group that did use the method took a little longer to read the passage than the students who did not use the method. However, the group using the method was able to restate precise facts, answer questions about the text, and understand the content, whereas the group that did not use the method could not answer many of the questions, and only understood the text superficially. This method may be taxing, but in the months leading up to the test, this method will help refocus the brain so that after numerous practices using the method, the students will be able to automatically use the method while taking the test and not have to do all of the steps.

The Steps

The first step in the Skill of Underlining is to take a ruler and put it directly under the line you are reading. Then, using the straight edge of the ruler, underline the entire line while reading it. Repeat this throughout the entire passage, underlining all of the lines of the passage. You will now have a basic understanding of the passage. At this point, you should go back to the beginning and restart the reading and underlining process again throughout the entire passage. Double underlining might seem repetitive and a waste of time, but the brain is now reabsorbing the information and processing what it only had one time to view. With the second reading completed, the brain can better understand the information in the passage. For the final step, once again reread the entire passage and with a highlighter; underline the main ideas, the buzzwords, proper nouns, and anything that pops up at you. With all the steps completed, you should answer the questions related to the text.

The Results

This process might seem lengthy, but those who follow the method have found that it works. Skipping any of the steps will not allow for maximum understanding. When taking the test, the student will not have to use the full method because by doing lots of practice questions before the test, the brain will understand how to read the text, comprehend it, and answer the questions. While taking the actual SAT® test, underline the lines of the passage once during the initial reading of the text; do not use the other steps. This method is a great study tool for a student's daily studies in all subjects.

> ## *Improving Reading Ability – On and Off the Test-*
> ## *~Basic Study Skills~*

Improving Reading Ability – off the test

When reading, select grade level, or reading level, books that are interesting. As you read each sentence, imagine the pictures in your head. Reading is not a race to finish the book as quickly as possible; reading is taking your time, digesting the ideas, and understanding the new ideas. As your reading speed and understanding get faster, you will begin to see the pictures in your mind appear with less effort. Also, in the margins of books, or a separate notebook, you can summarize entire paragraphs to get a better understanding of the text as a whole.

Step by step process to reading better

- Select a book and make a separate "SAT® Vocabulary" notebook; keep a pen and a dictionary at hand while reading.

- When you find a word you don't understand, write it in the notebook.

- Write down what you think the meaning of the word is, using context clues.

- Look up the word in the dictionary and write it in the notebook next to your guessed definition (or look it up on a dictionary app on your phone). Then, compare the two definitions. Were you close in your guess? If yes, you're good at this, if not, study and read more.

- Reread the sentence in the book replacing the word you don't know with the definition you looked up.

- Memorize the words you don't know. Use index cards or download the Anki flashcard program.

After reading and doing the above steps, read that selection once again, filling in the words' definitions. Your understanding and comprehension will increase because of these steps.

Improving Reading Comprehension Ability – on the test

Don't take your time on the test! Every second counts. That's why these books have been created to help you before you take the exam. When taking the test, if the question is an easy question, you will be able to answer it just because of its simplicity. Many SAT® test-takers will score around 1050, the national average, but to score higher than that and elevate yourself into the next tier, 1100 to 1200, you need to use a strategy. Use the PLAN Method (Page xii). Practice, learn and repeat to get better "on" the test.

The PLAN Method

The PLAN Method - Use a strategy to help you answer the questions, use PLAN (or sometimes PLAN"T")

By using the step by step PLAN method, you can systematically approach the questions that ordinarily might have stumped you, and eliminate answer choices to a more manageable guessing number. Though we are taught not to guess in school, students who score higher scores on the SAT® use some method that involves guessing on difficult questions.

P - Place your underlines. Unlike the Skill of Underlining, which is used to prepare for the test, underline words such as proper nouns, dates, years, and words or phrases that pop out at you because they are telling you something important. The questions on the test will usually be about something that is noteworthy, not something completely random and useless. These underlined areas will let you know where important information is, so when you return to find it, you'll have some memory of where to look.

L- Look for the **PAP**! (Prove-Answer-Phrase) The PAP is the answer to the question.

We can find the answers to the questions in the text itself. Whether it be a detail, an inference, a vocabulary, or author's style (author's purpose, author's meaning, author's tone, etc.) type question, the answer is somewhere in the passage, all that you need to do is find the Prove-Answer-Phrase, or PAP. The PAP is the word, phrase, clause, or sentence in the text that proves that one of the answer choices is the correct one. If you find the PAP, you most likely will be able to find the answer choice. If the question is a line reference question, the answer is usually at least one sentence above or one sentence below the sentence with the line reference in it, (sometimes two). It is not uncommon to have to read a whole paragraph to find and understand the text to answer the question. Find the PAP for each question, and you can get most of the questions correct.

For inference questions, you must look at the text around the idea that is being asked about in the question. Think about what the author is trying to hint at, and collect those hints if there are more than one. After that, with enough practice, you should be able to find the answer to the inference questions.

For vocabulary-based questions, if you're unsure of the word, look at the other words in the sentence, are they hinting that the word is positive, or negative? Use surrounding words to help determine what the word means. Also, knowing root words, prefixes, and suffixes are helpful in getting a feeling of the word without knowing its actual definition. A list of root words, prefixes, and suffixes is available at www.folpbooks.com to download for free. Still, knowing your vocab is key.

A - Answer the questions. Now you can answer the questions. When reading the text to answer the question, find the answer using as much of what you learned about the paired question elimination method as possible, but know that the answer to the question is quite often NOT on the line being referenced. The answer is usually at least one sentence above or one sentence below the sentence with the line reference in it. So, it is not uncommon to have to read a whole paragraph to find and understand the text to answer the question. Also, don't forget the Prove-Answer-Phrases to eliminate wrong answer choices, which allows you to focus on possible answer choices by clearing out the answer choices you know are wrong.

One simple elimination strategy is what some students began calling the "traffic light" system because there are three parts which tell you what to do, like a traffic light, which are:

X = wrong (Red light - stop)
• = maybe (Yellow light - start thinking whether to speed up or slow down, SLOW DOWN!)
√ = correct (Green light - go)

 As in the above <u>paired-question elimination method chart</u>, you can use the "traffic light" strategy to clear out wrong answer choices and leave yourself with possible correct answer choices, and frequently, the actual correct answer choice itself. You shouldn't do the traffic light strategy mentally; do it on the test paper so that you can actually see the Xs, •s, √s on the paper. During the test, test takers' minds race, making things confusing and leading to unnecessary mistakes.

N - No daydreaming! Keep your mind focused on the question at hand. If you feel your mind drifting while taking the test, don't lose valuable minutes that you need. Immediately snap out of your daze and refocus on the question.

*T - Time management. Keep the time. Each question should only take about 1 minute to answer, so don't let your time squander away. Use the rest of the PLAN(T) method, then move on after about a minute has passed.

 Finally, when you have finished all of the steps in this method, applied your own developed strategies (if you have any), and used common sense to eliminate, GUESS! Keep this very important point in mind while you take the test: you do not get points taken off for wrong answers, so make sure all of the bubbles are filled in on the answer sheet.

Big & Small Idea Practice Questions

Questions 1-2 are based on the following passage adapted from *Natural & Artificial Sewage Treatment by Lt. Col Alfred Jones.*

It is well known that land which is treated with sewage for the first time does not purify sewage so well as land that has been under systematic treatment for some time, and this is probably due to
5   the absorbing powers, which gradually ripen until they have reached their maximum of efficiency. This process of gradual improvement seems to be due to the formation of a slimy coating around each particle of soil, which growth does not only assist mechanical
10   filtration but also possesses high powers of absorbing oxygen. The depth to which polluting substances may penetrate into soil will probably differ in each case, but factors such as the velocity of the downward flow, the nature, and degree of the
15   polluting liquid, and the character of the soil may influence it. Where, therefore, the powers of the soil are overtaxed the polluting substances may reach the level of the underdrains and pass out through them, in which case the outflowing substance will be
20   but little better than the raw liquid. It must be the aim of careful management to avoid this.

1) The primary purpose of lines 1-6 is to

A) Define the usage of land for sewage purposes.
B) Inform on soil's ability to alter for better sewage take in.
C) Illustrate the powers of soil to adapt to different substances.
D) Explain about soil's conditions before and after treatment resulting in its change by substances.

2) The purpose of the passage as a whole is to

A) Explain the need for proper management of sewage.
B) Suggest ways that sewage can be filtered.
C) Give an explanation on how to better use soil to filter sewage.
D) Review an analysis of the land used for sewage and its effects.

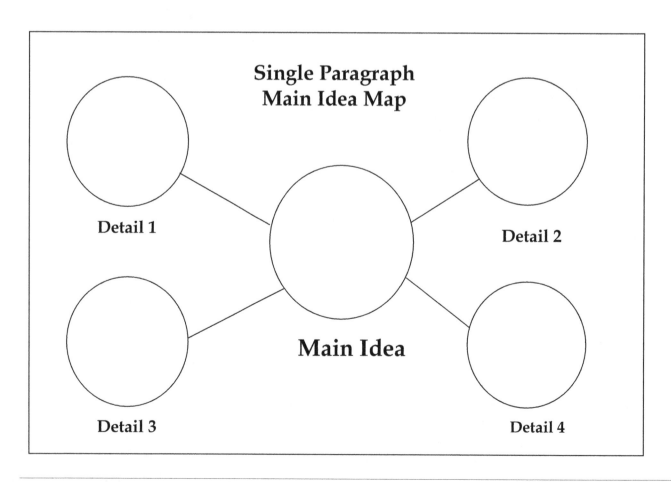

Single Paragraph
Main Idea Map

Detail 1

Detail 2

Main Idea

Detail 3

Detail 4

Questions 1-2 are based on the following passage adapted from *A Short History of the World* by H. G. Wells.

The Peace Conference at Versailles was a gathering very ill adapted to do more than carry out the conflicts and defeats of the war to their logical conclusions. The Germans, Austrians, Turks, and

5 Bulgarians were permitted no share in its deliberations; they were only to accept the decisions it dictated to them. From the point of view of human welfare, the choice of the place of meeting was particularly unfortunate. It was at Versailles in 1871

10 that, with every circumstance of triumphant vulgarity, the new German Empire had been proclaimed. The suggestion of a melodramatic reversal of that scene, in the same Hall of Mirrors, was overpowering.

15 1) The main purpose of the passage is to

A) Give an acknowledgment of an ineffectual cause.
B) Determine a new strategy for dealing with war.
C) Recognize a failed initiative.
D) Correct a faulty legal determination.

2) The last sentence of the passage mainly serves as

A) A rebuke of an embarrassment.
B) A criticism of underplaying an event.
C) An affirmation of wrongdoing.
D) An account of indifference.

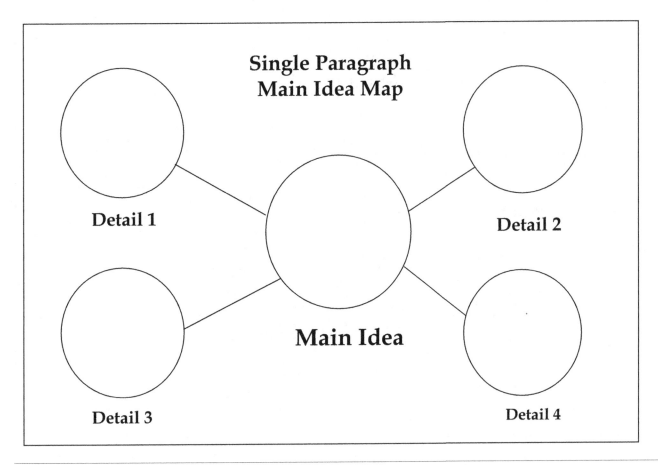

Single Paragraph Main Idea Map

Detail 1

Detail 2

Main Idea

Detail 3

Detail 4

Questions 1-2 are based on the following passage adapted from *the Story of Doctor Dolittle* by Hugh Lofting

Indeed, they had lost their way very badly. They had strayed a long way off the path, and the jungle was so thick with bushes and creepers and vines that sometimes they could hardly move at all, and the
5   Doctor had to take out his pocketknife and cut his way along. They stumbled into wet, boggy places; they got all tangled up in thick convolvulus runners; they scratched themselves on thorns, and twice they nearly lost the medicine bag in the underbrush.
10 There seemed no end to their troubles; and nowhere could they come upon a path. At last, after blundering about like this for many days, getting their clothes torn and their faces covered with mud, they walked right into the King's back garden by
15 mistake. The King's men came running up at once and caught them.

1) Over the course of the passage, the focus shifts from
A) An extreme situation to a mild one.
B) A disorienting situation to a terrible one.
C) An adventurous circumstance to a calm one.
D) A perplexing problem to an awry one.

2) The last sentence of the passage mainly serves to

A) Disclose sensitive information.
B) Inform of an ordeal.
C) Express worsening circumstances.
D) Elucidate on the group's deliverance.

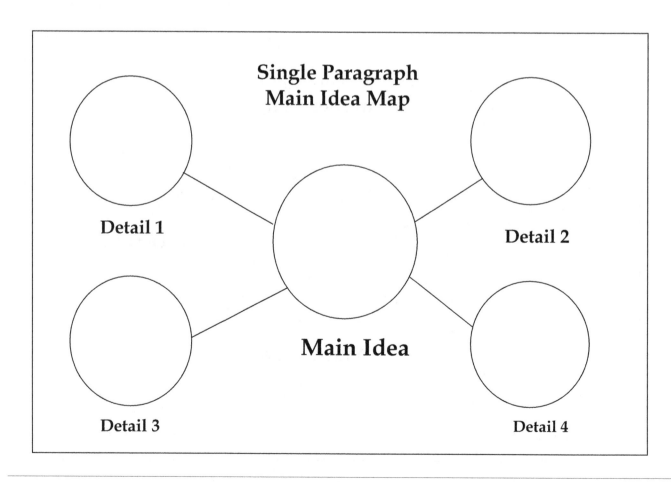

Questions 1-2 are based on the following passage adapted from The Fireside Chats of Franklin Delano Roosevelt.

First of all, let me state the simple fact that when you deposit money in a bank, the bank does not put the money into a safe deposit vault. It invests your money in many different forms of credit— bonds,
5 commercial paper, mortgages and many other kinds of loans. In other words, the bank puts your money to work to keep the wheels of industry and of agriculture turning around. A comparatively small part of the money you put into the bank is kept in
10 currency— an amount which in normal times is wholly sufficient to cover the cash needs of the average citizen. In other words, the total amount of all the currency in the country is only a small fraction of the total deposits in all of the banks.

1) Which choice best summarizes the passage?

A) A politician informing on the banking institution.
B) A president advising on how to invest money.
C) A head of state encouraging usage of banks.
D) A banker advising on how to save money.

2) The main purpose of lines 10-14 ("A comparatively ... citizen") is to

A) Illustrate the quantity of funds available in banks.
B) Inform of a dubious banking practice.
C) Describe inefficiencies of modern banking.
D) Explain how banks invest customers' money.

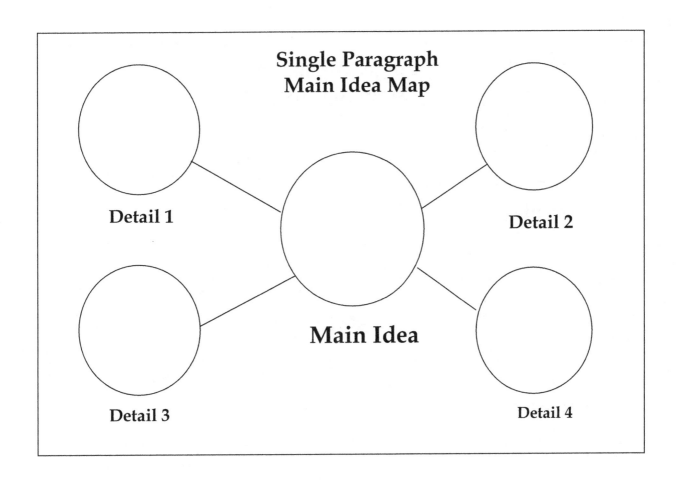

Single Paragraph Main Idea Map

Detail 1

Detail 2

Detail 3

Detail 4

Main Idea

Questions 1-2 are based on the following passage adapted from Voyager 1 Encounters Saturn by NASA.

No other generation has had the opportunity or the technology to reach beyond our world—to see, to touch, to hear the forces that shape our universe. In slightly over two decades, man has ingeniously

5 explored five distant planets—and two dozen moons. We have seen their weather and surfaces, landed on some, probed the atmospheres of others, and listened to their radio noises. Under the planetary exploration program of the National Aeronautics and

10 Space Administration, the Voyager Mission, begun in 1972, was designed to explore Jupiter, Saturn, their satellites, rings, magnetic fields, and interplanetary space. Two automated, reprogrammable spacecraft, Voyagers 1 and 2, were launched in late summer of

15 1977. Their goals: the outer planets.

1) The main purpose of the opening sentence of the passage is to

A) Pique the interest of the reader.
B) Divulge prior mission specifications.
C) Sensationalize about space exploration.
D) Emphasize the extent of NASA's accomplishments.

2) The main purpose of the passage is to

A) Illustrate the purpose of NASA.
B) Define NASA mission parameters.
C) Contrast the differences between two missions.
D) Inform of NASA's accomplishments.

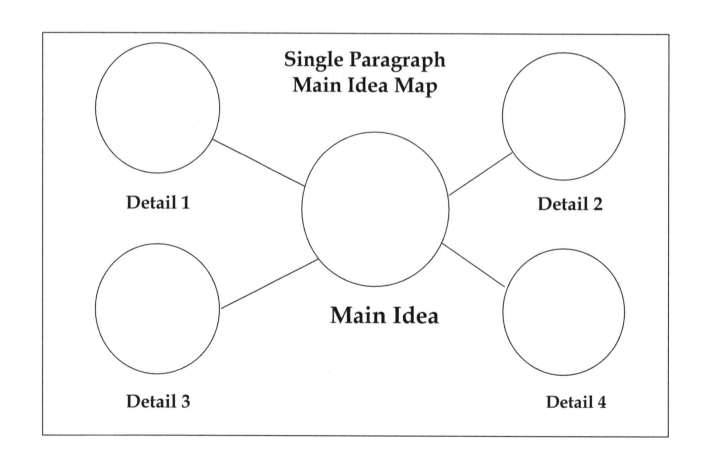

Questions 1-2 are based on the following passage adapted from *The Wonderful Wizard of Oz* by L. Frank Baum.

The cyclone had set the house down very gently--for a cyclone--in the midst of a country of marvelous beauty. There were lovely patches of greensward all about, with stately trees bearing rich and luscious
5   fruits. Banks of gorgeous flowers were on every hand, and birds with rare and brilliant plumage sang and fluttered in the trees and bushes. A little way off was a small brook, rushing and sparkling along between green banks, and murmuring in a voice very
10 grateful to a little girl who had lived so long on the dry, gray prairies.

1) The central idea of the paragraph is to

A) Develop the conflict of the story.
B) Inform the reader of the author's purpose.
C) Describe the effects of a natural disaster.
D) Illustrate the setting of the story.

2) What function do the words "The cyclone had set the house down very gently--for a cyclone"- in lines 1 and 2 serve?

A) They present a particular natural phenomenon.
B) They illustrate the cyclone's power.
C) They reveal the irregularity of a natural event.
D) They describe a consistency in the patterns of an immutable force.

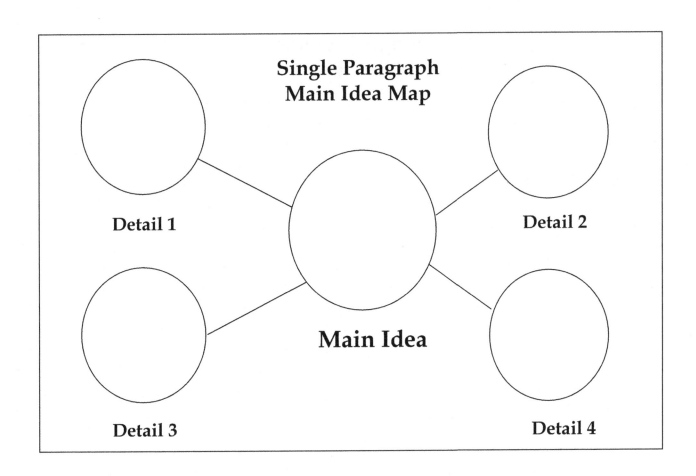

Single Paragraph Main Idea Map

Detail 1

Detail 2

Main Idea

Detail 3

Detail 4

Questions 1-2 are based on the following passage adapted from President Ronald Reagan's State of the Union Address.

Now we know that deficits are a cause for worry. But there's a difference of opinion as to whether taxes should be increased, spending cut, or some of both. Fear is expressed that government borrowing
5   to fund the deficit could inhibit the economic recovery by taking capital needed for business and industrial expansion. Well, I think that debate is missing an important point. Whether government borrows or increases taxes, it will be taking the same
10 amount of money from the private sector, and, either way, that's too much. Simple fairness dictates that government must not raise taxes on families struggling to pay their bills. The root of the problem is that government's share is more than we can
15 afford if we're to have a sound economy.

1) The central claim of the passage is that

A) The government should increase taxes.
B) The government should not increase taxes.
C) To pay for people's needs taxes should be imposed on industry.
D) The government needs to pay for people's needs.

2) The last sentence of the passage mainly serves to

A) Suggest the government must share more with the citizens.
B) Demand the economy must have more taxes.
C) Expose the government taxes too much.
D) Explain that people cannot afford to pay into a sound economy.

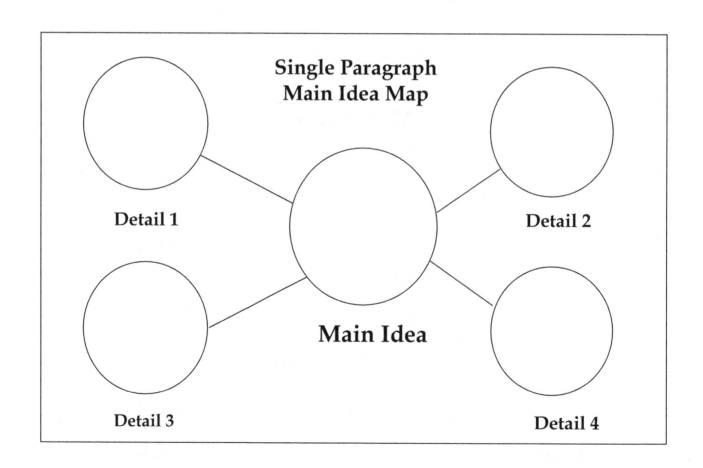

Questions 1-2 are based on the following passage adapted from Household Diary Summary, Mail Markets from http://about.usps.com/

The Household Diary Study examines mail by the markets it serves. This design cuts across classes, but provides a foundation for understanding mail flows and the marketplace changes that affect them.

5   Thirty-five percent of household mail contains correspondence and transactions, a share that is unchanged from 2011. In terms of volume, total correspondence fell 6.3 percent compared to 2011. Since 2002, correspondence fell 38 percent. In part,
10   the decline in correspondence is a continuation of long-term trends, but it is also strongly related to changing demographics and new technologies. Younger households send and receive fewer pieces of correspondence mail because they tend to be
15   early adaptors of new and faster communication media such as emails, social networking, and smartphones.

1) The first paragraph serves mainly to

A) Direct the reader to comprehend the mail system.
B) Note a change in mail distribution.
C) Describe different mail delivery options.
D) Present an overview of mail delivery.

2) The main idea of the second paragraph is

A) Reasons for differences in mail delivery.
B) Changes in USPS mail delivery protocol.
C) An explanation of the purpose of the USPS and its effects.
D) A breakdown of the reduction of mail delivery and its reasons.

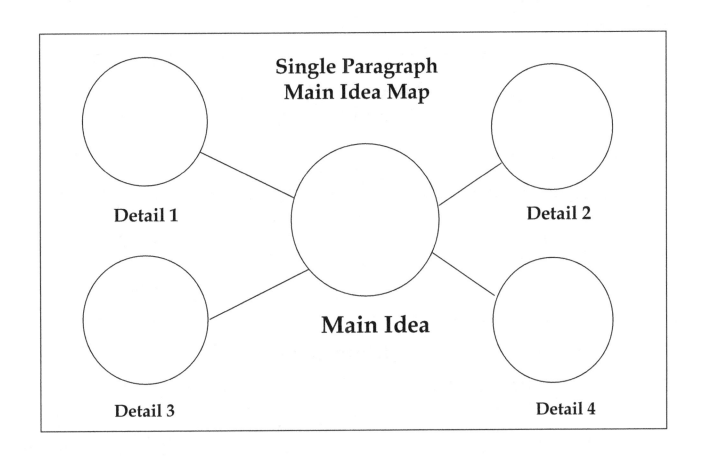

Single Paragraph Main Idea Map

Detail 1

Detail 2

Main Idea

Detail 3

Detail 4

Questions 1-2 are based on the following passage adapted from *Challenges for Uneven-Aged Silviculture in Restoration of Post-Disturbance Forests in Central Europe: A Synthesis,* an article published in *Forests Journal.*

The resistance and resilience of forest stands to disturbance are strongly influenced by forest management and the type of silvicultural system used. For example, forest stands managed with
5 uneven-aged silviculture generally create stands with small-scale heterogeneous structure and are thought to be both resistant and resilient to disturbance. In the context of this paper, the term uneven-aged silviculture refers to a range of
10 silvicultural systems that include single and group selection, irregular shelterwood, and freestyle systems. In continental Europe, this type of management, based on a liberal selection of felling regimes within the context of the aforementioned
15 systems, is often called close-to-nature silviculture. It has traditionally been used in many alpine countries, particularly in Switzerland, Slovenia, Italy, Austria, and parts of Germany, and more recently its use has become more widespread.

1) The main purpose of the opening sentence of the paragraph is to

A) Explain the reason for forest stands resistance and resilience to silvicultural systems.
B) Provide context to what a silviculture system is.
C) Disclose how forests affect change in the environment.
D) State how forest stands can remain healthy.

2) The central claim of the passage is that

A) Forest management and silvicultural systems being used are the best for forests' health.
B) Europe has used traditional systems to maintain strong forests.
C) Forestry systems in Europe are maintaining strong forests.
D) Silvicultural systems are expanding forests in Europe.

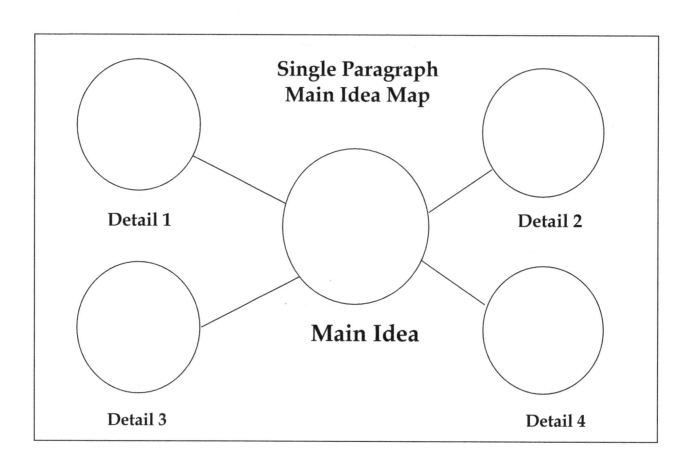

Single Paragraph
Main Idea Map

Detail 1

Detail 2

Main Idea

Detail 3

Detail 4

Questions 1-2 are based on the following passage adapted from *Adventures in American Bookshops, Antique Stores and Auction Rooms* by Guido Bruno

When a man has made money in America, he at once becomes a victim to the craze for an artistic home. The tradespeople with whom he comes in contact in order to achieve his artistic desires speak
5   of art and rugs and paintings. He reads in the newspapers about Mr. So-and-So who spent thousands of dollars for antique furniture or for pictures in auctions, and he begins his walks on these dangerous and costly grounds where one may buy
10 for goodly sums the ephemeral fame of a collector and a lover of objects of art. The reputation of an art expert seems to go with the objects as well as the wrapping paper and string.

It is the dream of every antique dealer once in his
15 life to enter one of those coveted garrets where treasures of six generations are stored in boxes, in cases and trunks. To enter this garret at the invitation of some real estate owner or lawyer who represents an estate anxious to sell the house and to
20 clear out the 'rubbish'; to buy the contents of such a garret for a few dollars and to find a painting by Rubens or Tintoretto or Martha Washington's wedding slippers or a suite of magnificent Colonial furniture ... sure enough, these are red-letter days
25 for almost every antique dealer.

1) During the course of the two paragraphs, the narrator's focus shifts from

A) An American's specific tastes to a house seller's preferences.
B) A fictional character to nonfictional characters.
C) A buyer to a seller.
D) The rich to the people who service the rich.

2) The main purpose of the final sentence of the second paragraph is to

A) Illustrate what an antique dealer acquires.
B) Describe the way an antique dealer acquires his items.
C) Explain steps for the acquisition of expensive items.
D) Advance the idea that an antique dealer's methods of attaining items are exhaustive.

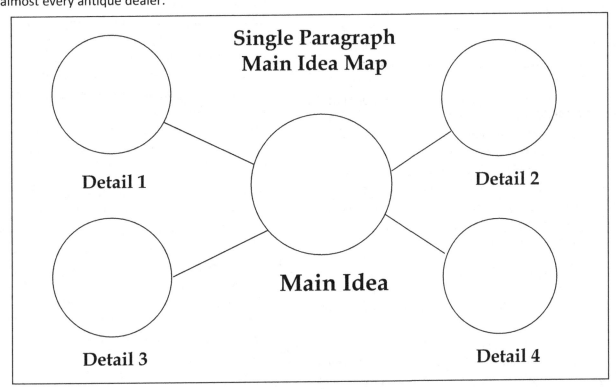

Single Paragraph Main Idea Map

Detail 1

Detail 2

Main Idea

Detail 3

Detail 4

Questions 1-6 are based on the following passage adapted from an essay by Ralph Waldo Emerson titled *Self-Reliance*.

There is a time in every man's education when he arrives at the conviction that envy is ignorance; that imitation is suicide; that he must take himself for better, for worse, as his portion; that though the
5 wide universe is full of good, no kernel of nourishing corn can come to him but through his toil bestowed on that plot of ground which is given to him to till. The power which resides in him is new in nature, and none but he knows what that is which he can do, nor
10 does he know until he has tried. Not for nothing one face, one character, one fact, makes much impression on him, and another none. This sculpture in the memory is not without preestablished harmony. The eye was placed where one ray should
15 fall, that it might testify of that particular ray. We but half express ourselves and are ashamed of that divine idea which each of us represents. It may be safely trusted as proportionate and of good issues, so it be faithfully imparted, but God will not have his
20 work made manifest by cowards. A man is relieved and happy when he has put his heart into his work and done his best, but what he has said or done otherwise shall give him no peace. It is a deliverance which does not deliver. In the attempt his genius
25 deserts him; no muse befriends; no invention, no hope.

Trust thyself: every heart vibrates to that iron string. Accept the place the divine providence has found for you, the society of your contemporaries,
30 the connection of events. Great men have always done so, and confided themselves childlike to the genius of their age, betraying their perception that the absolutely trustworthy was seated at their heart, working through their hands, predominating in all
35 their being. And we are now men, and must accept in the highest mind the same transcendent destiny; and not minors and invalids in a protected corner, not cowards fleeing before a revolution, but guides, redeemers, and benefactors, obeying the Almighty
40 effort, and advancing on Chaos and the Dark.

What pretty oracles nature yields us on this text, in the face and behavior of children, babes, and even brutes! That divided and rebel mind, that distrust of a sentiment because our arithmetic has computed
45 the strength and means opposed to our purpose, these have not. Their mind being whole, their eye is as yet unconquered, and when we look in their faces,

we are disconcerted. Infancy conforms to nobody: all conform to it so that one babe commonly makes
50 four or five out of the adults who prattle and play to it. So God has armed youth and puberty and manhood no less with its own piquancy and charm, and made it enviable and gracious and its claims not to be put by, if it will stand by itself. Do not think the
55 youth has no force, because he cannot speak to you and me. Hark! In the next room his voice is sufficiently clear and emphatic. It seems he knows how to speak to his contemporaries. Bashful or bold, then, he will know how to make us seniors very
60 unnecessary.

The nonchalance of boys who are sure of a dinner, and would disdain as much as a lord to do or say aught to conciliate one, is the healthy attitude of human nature. A boy is in the parlor what the pit is in
65 the playhouse; independent, irresponsible, looking out from his corner on such people and facts as pass by, he tries and sentences them on their merits, in the swift, summary way of boys, as good, bad, interesting, silly, eloquent, troublesome. He cumbers
70 himself never about consequences about interests; he gives an independent, genuine verdict. You must convince him: he does not convince you. But the man is, as it were, clapped into jail by his consciousness. As soon as he has once acted or
75 spoken with *éclat* he is a committed person, watched by the sympathy or the hatred of hundreds, whose affections must now enter into his account. There is no Lethe for this. Ah, that he could pass again into his neutrality! Who can thus avoid all pledges, and
80 having observed, observe again from the same unaffected, unbiased, unbribable, unaffrighted innocence, must always be formidable. He would utter opinions on all passing affairs, which being seen to be not private, but necessary, would sink like
85 darts into the ear of men, and put them in fear.

These are the voices which we hear in solitude, but they grow faint and inaudible as we enter into the world. Society everywhere is in conspiracy against the manhood of everyone of its members. Society is
90 a joint-stock company, in which the members agree, for the better securing of his bread to each shareholder, to surrender the liberty and culture of the eater. The virtue in most request is conformity. Self-reliance is its aversion. It loves not realities and
95 creators, but names and customs.

1) The passage primarily serves to

_____

_____

_____

_____

2) The second paragraph is primarily concerned with establishing

_____

_____

_____

_____

3) What function does the third paragraph serve in the passage as a whole?

_____

_____

_____

_____

4) During the course of the fourth paragraph, the author's focus shifts from

_____

_____

_____

5) The main purpose of lines 86-88 ("These ... world") is to

_____

_____

_____

_____

6) The last paragraph serves mainly to

_____

_____

_____

_____

Questions 1-6 are based on the following passage adapted from *Home Life of Great Authors with a focus on Washington Irving* by Hattie Tyng Griswold.

Washington Irving was born in the city of New York in 1783, the youngest of eleven children born to his parents. At that time New York was a rural city of twenty-three thousand inhabitants clustered about
5　the Battery. He was of a joyous and genial temperament, full of life and vivacity, and not at all inclined to religious seriousness. He was born with a passion for music and was also a great lover of the theatre. These things, in the eyes of his father, were
10　serious evils, and he felt great anxiety for the son's spiritual welfare. The gladsomeness and sportiveness of the boy's nature were things which he could not understand, and he feared that they were of the Evil One. There was no room in the darkness of his
15　religion's creed for anything that was simply bright and joyous. To save one's soul was the business of life; all things else were secondary and of small importance. Of course, he worried much over this handsome, dashing, susceptible, music-loving,
20　laughter-loving son, and doubtless shed many tears over his waywardness. Yet there was nothing wild about the boy. The writing of plays seems to have been his worst boyish offense. His first published writings were audacious satires upon the theatre,
25　the actors, and the local audiences. They had some promise and attracted some attention in the poverty of those times.

At the age of twenty-one, he was in such delicate health that a voyage to Europe was looked upon as
30　the only means of saving his life. He accordingly embarked for Bordeaux and made an extended tour of Europe, loitering in many places for weeks at a time, and laying up a store of memories which gave him pleasure throughout life. In Rome, he came
35　across Washington Allston, then unknown to fame. He was about three years older than Irving, and just establishing himself as a painter. Irving was completely captivated with the young Southerner, and they formed a very good friendship with each
40　other.

Irving even dreamed of remaining in Rome and turning artist himself that he might always be near his friend. He had a great dread of returning to the New World and settling down to the uncongenial
45　work of the law, and he fancied he had some talent for art. He certainly had one essential qualification,—a passionate love of color, and an eye for its harmonies. This love was a great source of pleasure to him throughout life. He always thought that he
50　might have succeeded as a landscape painter. However this might be, the gift of color-loving is in itself a rich endowment to any mind. There are few purer and higher sources of enjoyment in this life than this love of color, and it is a possession which
55　ought to be cultivated in every child.

But the art scheme was soon abandoned, and he went on to London, where he began his literary work. His name of Washington attracted considerable attention there, and he was frequently
60　asked if he was a relative of General Washington. A few years later, after he had written the "Sketch Book," two women were overheard in conversation near the bust of Washington in a large gallery. "Mother, who was Washington?" "Why, my dear,
65　don't you know?" was the reply, "he wrote the 'Sketch Book.'"

Soon after the book was published Irving was one night in the room with Mrs. Siddons, the Queen of Tragedy. She carried her tragic airs even into private
70　life, it is said, and when Irving was presented to her, he, being young and modest, was somewhat taken aback on being greeted with the single sentence, given in her grandest stage voice and with the loftiest stateliness, "You have made me weep." He
75　could find no words to reply and shrank away in silence. A very short time after he met with her again, and, although he sought to avoid her, she recognized him and repeated in tones as tragic as at first, "You have made me weep;" which salutation
80　had the effect of discomfiting Irving for the second time.

He returned to New York in 1806 and was much sought after in society from that time on. It was a very convivial company, that of old New York in the
85　early part of the century, and Irving entered into its pleasures with the rest of his friends living the good life.

1) The main purpose of the passage is to

_____

_____

_____

_____

2) The main purpose of lines 11-14 ("The ... One") is to

_____

_____

_____

3) During the course of the second paragraph, the narrator's focus shifts from

_____

_____

_____

4) The fourth paragraph is primarily concerned with

_____

_____

_____

5) The main idea of the fifth paragraph is that

_____

_____

_____

_____

6) The last sentence of the passage mainly serves to

_____

_____

_____

_____

Questions 1-6 are based on the following passage adapted from *The Extermination of The American Bison* by William T. Hornaday.

Of all the quadrupeds that have lived upon the earth, probably no other species has ever marshalled such innumerable hosts as those of the American bison. It would have been as easy to count or to
5 estimate the number of leaves in a forest as to calculate the number of buffaloes living at any given time during the history of the species previous to 1870. Even in South Central Africa, which has always been exceedingly prolific in great herds of game, it is
10 probable that all its quadrupeds taken together on an equal area would never have more than equalled the total number of buffalo in this country forty years ago.

Not only did the buffalo formerly range eastward
15 far into the forest regions of western New York, Pennsylvania, Virginia, the Carolinas, and Georgia, but in some places, it was so abundant as to cause remark. In the vicinity of the spot where the town of Clarion now stands, in north-western Pennsylvania,
20 Mr. Thomas Ashe relates that one of the first settlers built his log cabin near a salt spring which was visited by buffaloes in such numbers that "he supposed there could not have been less than two thousand in the neighborhood of the spring." During the first
25 years of his residence there, the buffaloes came in droves of about three hundred each Of the Blue Licks in Kentucky, Mr. John Filson thus wrote, in 1784: "The amazing herds of buffaloes which resort there, by their size and number, fill the traveler with
30 amazement and terror, especially when he beholds the prodigious roads they have made from all quarters, as if leading to some populous city; the vast space of land around these springs desolated as if by a ravaging enemy, and hills reduced to plains; for the
35 land near these springs is chiefly hilly. I have heard a hunter assert he saw above one thousand buffaloes at the Blue Licks at once; so numerous were they before the first settlers had wantonly sported away their lives." Col. Daniel Boone declared of the Red
40 River region in Kentucky, "The buffaloes were more frequent than I have seen cattle in the settlements, browsing on the leaves of the cane, or cropping the herbage of those extensive plains, fearless because ignorant of the violence of man. Sometimes we saw
45 hundreds in a drove, and the numbers about the salt springs were amazing." According to Ramsey, where

Nashville now stands, in 1770 there were "immense numbers of buffalo and other wild game. The country was crowded with them. Their bellowing
50 sounded from the hills and forest." Daniel Boone found vast herds of buffalo grazing in the valleys of East Tennessee, between the spurs of the Cumberland mountains.

Alas, this was not to be for much longer
55 throughout the lands this great beast once lived. A great extermination of this once innumerable species soon would decimate this species to nearly none. The causes which led to the practical extinction of the most economically valuable wild animal that ever
60 inhabited the American continent, are by no means obscure. It is well that we should know precisely what they were, and by the sad fate of the buffalo be warned in time against allowing similar causes to produce the same results with our elk, antelope,
65 deer, moose, caribou, mountain sheep, mountain goat, walrus, and other animals. It will be doubly deplorable if the remorseless slaughter we have witnessed during the last twenty years carries with it no lessons for the future. A continuation of the
70 record we have lately made as wholesale game butchers will justify posterity in dating us back with the mound builders and cave dwellers, when man's only known function was to slay and eat.

The primary cause of the buffalo's extermination,
75 and the one which embraced all others was the descent of civilization, with all its elements of destructiveness, upon the whole of the country inhabited by that animal. From the Great Slave Lake to the Rio Grande the home of the buffalo was
80 everywhere overrun by the man with a gun; and, as has ever been the case, the wild creatures were gradually swept away, the largest and most conspicuous forms being the first to go.

Other causes of the extermination of the buffalo
85 are man's reckless greed, his wanton destructiveness, and improvidence in not husbanding such resources as come to him from the hand of nature ready-made. Also, the total and utterly inexcusable absence of protective measures
90 and agencies on the part of the National Government and of the West States and Territories is to blame. Fault also lies on the beast itself because of its own stupidity of the animals themselves, and their indifference to man.

1) The main purpose of the passage is to

_____

_____

_____

_____

2) The main purpose of the opening sentence of the passage is to

_____

_____

_____

_____

3) What function does the second paragraph serve in the passage as a whole?

_____

_____

_____

4) The main purpose of lines 54-55 ("Alas...lived) is to

_____

_____

_____

_____

5) The primary function of the fourth and fifth paragraphs is to

_____

_____

_____

_____

6) Over the course of the passage, the focus shifts from

_____

_____

_____

_____

Questions 1-6 are based on the following passage adapted from *The Chemistry of Food and Nutrition* by A.W. Duncan, F.C.S.

We may define a food to be any substance which will repair the functional waste of the body, increase its growth, or maintain the heat, muscular, and nervous energy. In its most comprehensive sense,
5 the oxygen of the air is a food; as although it is admitted by the lungs, it passes into the blood and there reacts upon the other food which has passed through the stomach. It is usual, however, to restrict the term food to such nutriment as enters the body
10 by the intestinal canal. Water is often spoken of as being distinct from food, but for this, there is no sufficient reason. Water forms an essential part of all the tissues of the body. It is the solvent and carrier of other substances.

15 Many popular writers have divided foods into flesh-formers, heat-givers, and bone-formers. Although attractive from its simplicity, this classification will not bear criticism. Flesh-formers are also heat-givers. Only a portion of the mineral
20 matter goes to form bone.

Mineral matter, or salts, is left as ash when food is thoroughly burnt. The most important salts are calcium phosphate, carbonate and fluoride, sodium chloride, potassium phosphate and chloride, and
25 compounds of magnesium, iron, and silicon. Mineral matter is quite as necessary for plant as for animal life, and is therefore present in all food, except in the case of some highly prepared ones, such as sugar, starch, and oil. Children require a good proportion of
30 calcium phosphate for the growth of their bones, while adults require less. The outer part of the grain of cereals is the richest in mineral constituents; white flour and rice are deficient. Wheatmeal and oatmeal are especially recommended for the
35 quantity of phosphates and other salts contained in them. Mineral matter is necessary not only for the bones but for every tissue of the body.

When haricots are cooked, the liquid is often thrown away, and the beans served nearly dry, or
40 with parsley or other sauce. Not only is the food less tasty but important saline constituents are lost. The author has made the following experiments:—German whole lentils, Egyptian split red lentils, and medium haricot beans were soaked all night, 16

45 hours, in just sufficient cold water to keep them covered. The water was poured off and evaporated, the residue heated in the steam oven to perfect dryness and weighed. After pouring off the water, the haricots were boiled in more water until
50 thoroughly cooked, the liquid kept as low as possible. The liquid was poured off as clear as possible, from the haricots, evaporated and dried. The ash was taken in each case, and the alkalinity of the water soluble ash was calculated as potash, K_2O.
55 The quantity of water which could be poured off was with the German lentils, half as much more than the original weight of the pulse; not quite as much could be poured off the others.

The loss on soaking in cold water, unless the water
60 is preserved, is seen to be considerable. The split lentils, having had the protecting skin removed, lose most. In every case, the ash contained a good deal of phosphate and lime. Potatoes are rich in important potash salts; by boiling a large quantity is lost, by
65 steaming less and by baking in the skins, scarcely any. The flavor is also much better after baking. The usual addition of common salt, sodium chloride, to boiled potatoes is no proper substitute for the loss of their natural saline constituents. Natural and
70 properly cooked foods are so rich in sodium chloride and other salts that the addition of common salt is unnecessary. An excess of the latter excites thirst and spoils the natural flavor of the food. It is the custom, especially in restaurants, to add a large
75 quantity of salt to pulse, savory food, potatoes, and soups. Bakers' brown bread is usually very salty, and sometimes white is also. In some persons, much salt causes irritation of the skin, and the writer has knowledge of the salt food of vegetarian restaurants
80 causing or increasing dandruff. As a rule, fondness for salt is an acquired taste, and after its discontinuance for a time, food thus flavored becomes unpalatable.

1) The central claim of the passage is that

_____

_____

_____

_____

2) The main purpose of lines 8-10 ("It ... canal") is to

_____

_____

_____

3) During the course of the third paragraph, the narrator's focus shifts from

_____

_____

_____

4) The main purpose of the fourth paragraph is to

_____

_____

_____

5) The central problem that Duncan describes in the passage is that water

_____

_____

_____

6) The main idea of the final paragraph is that

_____

_____

_____

Questions 1-6 are based on the following passage adapted from *Great Men and Famous Women* by Charles F. Horne

William I., King of England, surnamed the Conqueror, was born in 1027 or 1028. He was the son of Robert, Duke of Normandy and Herleva, daughter of Fulbert, a tanner of Falaise. When he
5 was about seven years old, his father, intending to go on pilgrimage and having no legitimate sons, proposed him as his heir. The great men of the duchy did homage to the child, and a year later his father's death left him to make good his claim. Anarchy was
10 the natural result of a minority. William's life was on more than one occasion in danger, and several of his guardians perished in his service. At the earliest possible age, he received knighthood from the hands of Henry I. of France and speedily began to show
15 signs of his capacity for government.

In 1042 he insisted that the "truce of God" should be proclaimed and observed in Normandy. When he was about twenty years old his authority was threatened by a general conspiracy, which spread
20 through the western half of his duchy. An attempt was made to seize him at Valognes, and he only escaped by riding hard all night to his own castle at Falaise. Bessin and Cotentin, the most Norman parts of Normandy, rose in rebellion. William sought and
25 obtained aid from King Henry, and completely defeated the rebels at Val-es-Dunes near Caen. The battle was but a combat of horse, but it decided the fate of the war and left William master of his duchy. The debt which he owed to Henry was repaid next
30 year. War broke out between Geoffrey, Count of Anjou, and Henry, and William came to his suzerain's assistance. Alençon, one of the chief border fortresses between Normandy and Maine, which had received an Angevin garrison, was captured by the
35 duke. The inhabitants had taunted him with his birth, and William, who had dealt leniently with the rebels after Val-es-Dunes, took a cruel revenge. Soon afterward Domfront, another important border fortress, fell into his hands.

40 William visited England in 1051 where he met Matilda, daughter of Baldwin, Earl of Flanders, and a descendant of Alfred, whom two years later he married. The marriage had been forbidden by a council at Rheims as uncanonical and was opposed
45 by Lanfranc, Prior of Bec. This produced a quarrel between Lanfranc and William, who ravaged the lands of the abbey and ordered the banishment of its prior. Lanfranc, however, Lanfranc soon came to terms with the duke, and engaged to obtain a
50 dispensation from Rome, which, however, was not granted till 1059.

Strengthened by this alliance with Flanders, William showed himself more than a match for all his enemies. Henry, who had hitherto been for the most
55 part friendly, now turned against him. After the suppression of some isolated revolts, William was threatened in 1054 by a great confederacy. His dominions were invaded by the forces of the French king, in combination with those of Geoffrey of Anjou,
60 Theobald of Blois, and others. William remained at first on the defensive; then, falling suddenly on one of the French armies at Mortemer, in the northeastern corner of his duchy, he cut it to pieces. This blow put an end to the war; Henry made peace, and
65 William took the opportunity of extending his dominions in a southerly direction. He built fresh fortresses and exacted homage from Count Geoffrey of Mayenne.

In 1058 Henry and Count Geoffrey made a final
70 effort to crush their dangerous neighbor; but the effort failed, like those which preceded it. William again allowed the allies to enter and ravage his territory; but, while the French army was crossing the Dive at Varaville, he attacked and completely
75 destroyed their rear guard, which was cut off from the van by the advancing tide. Henry again made peace, and soon afterward died (1060). The death of Geoffrey of Anjou in the same year relieved William of his most formidable rival for the possession of
80 Maine. Herbert Wake-Dog, the lawful ruler of that territory, who had been dispossessed by Geoffrey, recovered his dominions on the latter's death. He at once "commended" himself to William, thus making the duke his heir. On his death in 1063, William took
85 possession of Le Mans and the county of which it was the capital—an acquisition which extended his southern frontier nearly to the Loire. Yet these victories were small compared to his greatest victory: the invasion and conquering of England.

1) The main purpose of the passage is to

_____

_____

_____

_____

2) The main purpose of the lines 4-7 ("When...heir") of the passage is to

_____

_____

_____

3) What function does the second paragraph serve in the passage as a whole?

_____

_____

_____

_____

4) The primary function of the third paragraph is to

_____

_____

_____

_____

5) The main purpose of lines 56-59 ("His ...others) is to

_____

_____

_____

_____

6) The primary function of the fourth and fifth paragraphs is to

_____

_____

_____

Questions 1-5 are based on the following passage adapted from *Proverbs and Their Lessons* by Richard Chenevix Trench.

It is very likely that for some of us, proverbs have never attracted the notice which I am persuaded they deserve; and from this, it may follow that, when invited to bestow even a brief attention on them, we
5 are in some doubt whether they will repay our pains. We think of them but as sayings on the lips of the multitude; not a few of them have been familiar to us as far back as we can remember; often employed by ourselves, or in our hearing, on slight and trivial
10 occasions. Thus, from these and other causes, it may very well be, that, however sometimes one may have taken our fancy, we yet have remained blind in the main to the wit, wisdom, and imagination, of which they are full; and very little conscious of the
15 amusement, instruction, insight, which they are capable of yielding. Unless too we have devoted a certain attention to the subject, we shall not be at all aware how little those more familiar ones, which are frequent on the lips of men, exhaust the treasure of
20 our native proverbs. How many and what excellent ones remain behind, having now for the most part fallen out of sight; or what riches in like kind other nations possess. We may little guess how many aspects of interest there are in which our own by
25 themselves, and our own compared with those of other people, may be regarded.

And yet there is much to induce us to reconsider our judgment, should we be thus tempted to slight them, and to count them not merely trite, but trivial
30 and unworthy of serious attention. The fact that they please the people, and have pleased them for ages is indisputable. They possess so vigorous a principle of life, as to have maintained their ground, ever new and ever young, through all the centuries of a
35 nation's existence, nay, that many of them have pleased not one nation only, but many, so that they have made themselves a home in the most different lands. Further, that they have, not a few of them, come down to us from the remotest antiquity, borne
40 safely upon the waters of that great stream of time, which has swallowed so much beneath its waves. All this, I think, may well make us pause, should we be tempted to turn away from them with anything of indifference or disdain.

45 And then further, there is this to be considered, that some of the greatest poets, the most profound philosophers, the most learned scholars, the most genial writers in every kind, have delighted in them, have made large and frequent use of them, have
50 bestowed infinite labour on the gathering and elucidating of them. In a fastidious age, indeed, and one of false refinement, they may go nearly or quite out of use among the so-called upper classes. No gentleman, says Lord Chesterfield, or "no man of
55 fashion," as I think is his exact phrase, "ever uses a proverb."

Proverbs have always been dear to the true intellectual aristocracy of a nation; there is abundant evidence to prove. Take but these three names in
60 evidence, which though few, are in themselves a host. Aristotle made a collection of proverbs; nor did he count that he was herein doing aught unworthy of his great reputation, however, some of his adversaries may afterwards have made of the fact
65 that he did so an imputation against him. He is said to have been the first collector of them, though many afterwards followed in the same path. Shakespeare loves them so well, that besides often citing them, and scattering innumerable covert
70 allusions, rapid side glances at them, which we are in danger of missing unless at home in the proverbs of England, several of his plays, as *Measure for Measure, All's well that ends well*, have popular proverbs for their titles. And Cervantes, a name only
75 inferior to Shakespeare, has made very plain the affection with which he regarded them. Every reader of *Don Quixote* will remember his squire, who sometimes cannot open his mouth but there drop from it almost as many proverbs as phrases. I might
80 name others who have held the proverb in honor— men who, though they may not attain to these first three, are yet deservedly accounted great; as Plautus, the most genial of Latin poets, Rabelais and Montaigne, the two most original of French authors;
85 and how often Fuller, whom Coleridge has styled the wittiest of writers, justifies this praise in his witty employment of some old proverb. No reader can thoroughly understand and enjoy *Hudibras*, none but will miss a multitude of its keenest allusions, who is
90 not thoroughly familiar with the proverbial literature of England.

1) The main purpose of the passage is to

A) Emphasize the value of proverbs on education.
B) Highlight the importance of knowing proverbs.
C) Explain why proverbs are good to know.
D) Describe the reasons proverbs are important.

2) The main purpose of the first paragraph is to emphasize that

A) People do not know the meanings of proverbs.
B) The average person knows proverbs, but not the depth of them.
C) People would benefit from knowing proverbs.
D) Other nations' proverbs may be as beneficial as our own.

3) The primary purpose of the first sentence in paragraph 2 is to establish that

A) Proverbs can induce wisdom.
B) To most people, proverbs are unnecessary.
C) Proverbs should not be thought of as commonplace.
D) People should know proverbs.

4) During the course of the third paragraph, the narrator's focus shifts from

A) Academic ideas to gentlemen's habits.
B) Intellectuals' proverb usage to the wealthy's disdain for them.
C) Poets' preferences for proverbs to the upper-classes' disuse.
D) A nobleman's views to a scholar's preferences.

5) The main idea of the final paragraph is to

A) Highlight Aristotle, Shakespeare, and Cervantes' usage of proverbs.
B) Support the third paragraph by naming people of renown.
C) Counter the third paragraph's statement that the upper-classes did not use proverbs by giving examples of those who did.
D) Counter the idea that only the higher people in society use proverbs.

Questions 1-5 are based on the following passage adapted from *The History of Woman Suffrage Vol 1.*

In gathering up the threads of history in the last century, and weaving its facts and philosophy together, one can trace the liberal social ideas, growing out of the political and religious revolutions
5 in France, Germany, Italy, and America. Their tendency to substitute for the divine right of kings, priests, and orders of nobility, the higher and broader one of individual conscience and judgment in all matters pertaining to this life and that which is
10 to come. It is not surprising that in so marked a transition period from the old to the new, as seen in the eighteenth century, that women, trained to think and write and speak, should have discovered that they, too, had some share in the newborn liberties
15 suddenly announced to the world. That the radical political theories, propagated in different countries, made their legitimate impress on the minds of women of the highest culture, is clearly proved by their writings and conversation. While in their
20 ignorance, women are usually more superstitious, more devoutly religious than men; those trained to thought, have generally manifested more interest in political questions, and have more frequently spoken and written on such themes, than on those merely
25 religious. This may be attributed, in a measure, to the fact that the tendency of woman's mind, at this stage of her development, is toward practical, rather than toward speculative science.

Questions of political economy lie within the realm
30 of positive knowledge; those of theology belongs to the world of mysteries and abstractions, which those minds, only, that imagine they have compassed the known, are ambitious to enter and explore. And yet, the quickening power of the Protestant Reformation
35 roused woman, as well as man, to new and higher thought. The bold declarations of Luther, placing individual judgment above church authority, the faith of the Quaker that the inner light was a better guide than arbitrary law, the religious idealism of the
40 Transcendentalists, and their teachings that souls had no gender, had each a marked influence in developing woman's self-assertion. Such ideas making all divine revelations as veritable and momentous to one soul, as another, tended directly
45 to equalize the members of the human family, and place men and women on the same plane of moral responsibility.

The revelations of science, too, analyzing and portraying the wonders and beauties of this material
50 world, crowned with new dignity, man and woman, nature's last and proudest work. Combe and Spurzheim, proving by their phrenological discoveries that the feelings, sentiments, and affections of the soul, mould and shape the skull,
55 gave new importance to woman's thought as mother of the race. Thus, each new idea in religion, politics, science, and philosophy, tending to individualism, rather than authority, came into the world freighted with new hopes of liberty for woman.

60 And when in the progress of civilization, the time had fully come for the recognition of the feminine element in humanity, women, in every civilized country unknown to each other, began simultaneously to demand a broader sphere of
65 action. Thus, the first public demand for political equality by a body of women in convention assembled, was a link in the chain of woman's development, binding the future with the past, as complete and necessary in itself, as the events of any
70 other period of her history. The ridicule of facts does not change their character. Many who study the past with interest, and see the importance of seeming trifles in helping forward great events, often fail to understand some of the best pages of history made
75 under their own eyes. Hence the woman suffrage movement has not yet been accepted as the legitimate outgrowth of American ideas—a component part of the history of our republic—but is falsely considered the wilful outburst of a few
80 unbalanced minds, whose ideas can never be realized under any form of government.

Among the immediate causes that led to the demand for the equal political rights of women in this country, three of significant importance can be
85 noted. State legislatures discussed the property of married women which became privy to the press, then to the dinner table. Francis Wright wrote an educational book on politics, religion, and social ideas leading many to side with the cause of
90 suffrage. Lastly was the effect of the Anti-slavery movement gathering its eloquent speakers, ablest logicians, and high morality men and women who also agreed with our great cause.

1) The central claim of the passage is that

A) Many movements have led to the strong support of the women's suffrage movement.
B) The women's suffrage movement is important for women to attain voting rights.
C) A history of the ideas leading to the women's suffrage movement.
D) People's inevitable realization that the women's suffrage movement must come to a reality.

2) The main purpose of lines 1-10 "(In... come")" is to

A) Present that liberal social ideas cause changes in ideas.
B) Illustrate that nations are affected by philosophical theories.
C) Describe how individualism replaces authoritarian structures.
D) Show that history proves that the suffrage movement will eventually come about.

3) The central idea of the third paragraph is that

A) Woman's liberty should be achieved as women are the formative element in humans.
B) Science is proving that women are important, and thus should have voting rights.
C) Certain scientific theories state that woman is significant in the formation of humans.
D) Woman is foundational in the forming of the human spirit according to science.

4) The main purpose of the last paragraph is to

A) Define the author's ideas of the women's suffrage movement.
B) Clarify the author's ideas of why the women's suffrage movement will happen.
C) Explain the reasons for the insistence of women's suffrage.
D) Elaborate on the causes of women's suffrage.

5) Over the course of the passage, the focus shifts from

A) The foundational ideas of individualism to their impetus on women's suffrage.
B) The history of women's suffrage to the formation of the women's suffrage movement.
C) The identification of key philosophical factors to the women's suffrage movement's conception.
D) Several different philosophies inspiring the women's suffrage movement.

Questions 1-5 are based on the following passage is adapted from *Distribution of Animals* by Alfred Russel Wallace.

Although birds are, of all land vertebrates, the best able to cross seas and oceans, it is remarkable how closely the main features of their distribution correspond with those of the mammals. South
5 America possesses the low Formicaroid type of Passeres, the largest order of birds, which, compared with the more highly developed forms of the Eastern Hemisphere, is analogous to the Cebidæ and Hapalidæ, two New World monkey families, as
10 compared with the Old World Apes and Monkeys. While Cracidæ, a South American bird family, as compared with the pheasants and grouse, a type of game bird, may be considered parallel to the Edentata, mammals like sloths and anteaters, as
15 compared with the Ungulates, hoofed animals, of the Old World. The marsupials of America and Australia, are paralleled among birds, in the Struthionidæ, like ostriches, and Megapodiidæ, chickens and such birds; the Lemurs and Insectivora
20 preserved in Madagascar are represented by the Mascarene Raphinae

From these and many other similarities of distribution, it is clear that birds have, as a rule, followed the same great lines of migration as
25 mammals; and that oceans, seas, and deserts, have always to a great extent limited their range. Yet these barriers have not been absolute, and in the course of ages, birds have been able to reach almost every habitable land upon the globe. Hence have
30 arisen some of the most curious and interesting phenomena of distribution; and many islands, which are entirely destitute of mammals, or possess a very few species, abound in birds, often of peculiar types and remarkable for some unusual character or habit.
35 Striking examples of such interesting bird faunas are those of New Zealand, the Sandwich Islands, the Galapagos, the Mascarene Islands, the Moluccas, and the Antilles. Even small and remote islets, such as Juan Fernandez and Norfolk Island, have more
40 light thrown upon their history by means of their birds, than by any other portion of their scanty fauna.

Another peculiar feature in the distribution of this class is the extraordinary manner in which certain groups and certain external characteristics, have
45 become developed in islands, where the smaller and less powerful birds have been protected from the incursions of mammal enemies, and where rapacious birds—which seem to some degree dependent on the abundance of mammals—are also scarce. Thus,
50 we have the pigeons and the parrots most wonderfully developed in the Australian region, which is preeminently insular; and both these groups here acquire conspicuous colors very unusual, or altogether absent, elsewhere. Similar colors, black
55 and red, appear, in the same two groups, in the distant Mascarene Islands; while in the Antilles the parrots often have white heads, a characteristic not found in the allied species on the South American continent. Crests, too, are largely developed, in both
60 these groups, in the Australian region only; and a crested parrot formerly lived in Mauritius,—a coincidence too much like that of the colors as above noted, to be considered accidental.

Again, birds exhibit to us a remarkable contrast as
65 regards the oceanic islands of tropical and temperate latitudes; while most of the former present hardly any cases of specific identity with the birds of adjacent continents, the latter often show hardly any differences. The Galapagos and Madagascar are
70 examples of the first named peculiarity; the Azores and the Bermudas of the last; and the difference can be clearly traced to the frequency and violence of storms in the one case and to the calms or steady breezes in the other.

75 It appears then, that although birds do not afford us the same convincing proof of the former union of now disjoined lands as we obtain from mammals, yet they give us much curious and suggestive information as to the various and complex modes in
80 which the existing peculiarities of the distribution of animals have been brought about. They also throw much light on the relationship between distribution and the external characters of animals.

1) Which choice best summarizes the passage?

A) The similarities of birds and mammals of certain regions.
B) The differences of island birds from their mammal counterparts.
C) Birds have evolved differently as a result of migrating to secluded islands.
D) Birds are changing due to evolutionary isolation in many parts of the world.

2) What function does the first paragraph serve in the passage as a whole?

A) It establishes that birds and mammals in certain areas relate to the presence of other types of animals in that same area.
B) It acknowledges that some birds can travel over vast physical boundaries.
C) It illustrates that birds and mammals are distributed throughout the world.
D) It claims that birds resemble the mammals of certain areas.

3) The last sentence of paragraph two mainly serves to

A) Express the author's feelings about fauna.
B) Make a declaration of an impact birds made.
C) Identify a shift in the subject of the paragraph.
D) Introduce a difference in birds and fauna.

4) Over the course of the third paragraph, the focus shifts from

A) A criticism of a disputed fact to a new theory.
B) A description to its likely cause.
C) An explanation to examples.
D) An account to a result.

5) The main idea of the final paragraph is that

A) Birds can disclose much about the world.
B) Birds reveal much from their dispersion and related effects of it.
C) Birds and mammals are distributed and have equal value.
D) Birds are present where mammals are absent and have similarities to mammals.

Questions 1-5 are based on the following passage adapted from an essay titled *Economy* by Henry David Thoreau

I sometimes wonder that we can be so frivolous, I may almost say, as to attend to the gross but somewhat foreign form of servitude called Negro Slavery. There are so many keen and subtle masters
5   that enslave both North and South. It is hard to have a Southern overseer; it is worse to have a Northern one, but worst of all when you are the slave driver of yourself.

10   Talk of a divinity in man! Look at the teamster on the highway, wending to market by day or night; does any divinity stir within him? His highest duty to fodder and water his horses! What is his destiny to him compared with the shipping interests? Does not
15   he drive for Squire Make-a-stir? How godlike, how immortal, is he? See how he cowers and sneaks, how vaguely all the day he fears, not being immortal nor divine, but the slave and prisoner of his own opinion of himself, a fame won by his own deeds. Public
20   opinion is a weak tyrant compared with our own private opinion.

What a man thinks of himself, that it is which determines, or rather indicates, his fate. Self-
25   emancipation even in the West Indian provinces of the fancy and imagination, - what Wilberforce is there to bring that about? Think, also, of the ladies of the land weaving toilet cushions against the last day, not to betray too green an interest in their fates! As
30   if you could kill time without injuring eternity.

The mass of men lead lives of quiet desperation. What is called resignation is confirmed desperation. From the desperate city, you go into the desperate country, and have to console yourself with the
35   bravery of minks and muskrats. A stereotyped but unconscious despair is concealed even under what are called the games and amusements of mankind. There is no play in them, for this comes after work.
40   But it is a characteristic of wisdom not to do desperate things.

When we consider what, to use the words of the catechism, is the chief end of man, and what are the true necessaries and means of life, it appears as if
45   men had deliberately chosen the common mode of living because they preferred it to any other. Yet they honestly think there is no choice left. But alert and healthy natures remember that the sun rose clear. It is never too late to give up our prejudices.
50   No way of thinking or doing, however ancient, can be trusted without proof. What everybody echoes or in silence passes by as true today may turn out to be falsehood tomorrow, mere smoke of opinion, which some had trusted for a cloud that would sprinkle
55   fertilizing rain on their fields.

What old people say you cannot do, you try and find that you can. Old deeds for old people, and new deeds for new. Old people did not know enough
60   once, perchance, to fetch fresh fuel to keep the fire agoing; new people put a little dry wood under a pot, and are whirled around the globe with the speed of birds, in a way to kill old people, as the phrase is. Age is no better, hardly so well, qualified for an instructor
65   as youth, for it has not profited so much as it has lost. One may almost doubt if the wisest man has learned anything of absolute value by living. Practically, the old have no very important advice to give the young, their own experience has been so partial, and their
70   lives have been such miserable failures, for private reasons, as they must believe; and it may be that they have some faith left which belies that experience, and they are only less young than they were. I have lived some thirty years on this planet,
75   and I have yet to hear the first syllable of valuable or even earnest advice from my seniors. They have told me nothing and probably cannot tell me anything to the purpose. Here is life, an experiment to a great extent untried by me; but it does not avail me that
80   they have tried it. If I have any experience which I think valuable, I am sure to reflect that of this, my mentors said nothing about to me.

One farmer says to me, "You cannot live on
85   vegetable food solely, for it furnishes nothing to make bones with"; and so he religiously devotes a part of his day to supplying his system with the raw material of bones; walking all the while he talks behind his oxen, which, with vegetable made bones,
90   jerk him and his lumbering plow along in spite of every obstacle. Some things are really necessaries of life in some circles, the most helpless and diseased, which in others are luxuries merely, and in others still are entirely unknown.

1) One central idea of the passage is that

A) Man should be confident and live deliberately.
B) Man should not be a slave.
C) How man thinks of himself is how he will live.
D) Man must live according to society's expectations.

2) The last sentence of the second paragraph mainly serves to show that

A) Public opinion is not strong against a tyrant.
B) Towards government, the public holds a stronger opinion rather than private opinions.
C) People's opinions of themselves are more critical than how others form opinions of us.
D) People's opinions of us are stronger than our own of ourselves.

3) The primary function of the second and third paragraphs is to

A) Elaborate on the first paragraph's main idea.
B) Question the purpose of man's existence.
C) Compare ideas on man's identity.
D) Contrast opposing ideas.

4) The central idea that Thoreau describes in the sixth paragraph is that

A) There is nothing to learn from old people.
B) Old people have not enough knowledge to convey to those who are younger.
C) His experiences with old people have been advantageous.
D) The youth can gain much from old people's knowledge.

5) The primary function of the final paragraph is to

A)   Summarize the passage.
B)   Describe a false premise.
C)   Illustrate a statement with an example.
D)   Explain a dichotomy of opinion.

Questions 1-5 are based on the following passage adapted from an essay titled *Reconstruction* by Frederick Douglass.

There is cause to be thankful even for rebellion. It is an impressive teacher, though a stern and terrible one. In both characters, it has come to us, and it was perhaps needed in both. It is an instructor never a
5 day before its time, for it comes only when all other means of progress and enlightenment have failed. Whether the oppressed and despairing bondman, no longer able to repress his deep yearnings for manhood, or the tyrant, in his pride and impatience,
10 takes the initiative and strikes the blow for a firmer hold and a longer lease of oppression, the result is the same,—society is instructed.

It is obvious to common sense that the rebellious states stand today, in point of law, precisely where
15 they stood when, exhausted, beaten, conquered, they fell powerless at the feet of Federal authority. Their state governments were overthrown, and the lives and property of the leaders of the Rebellion were forfeited. In reconstructing the institutions of
20 these shattered and overthrown states, Congress should begin with a clean slate, and make clean work of it.

It is not, however, within the scope of this paper to point out the precise steps to be taken, and the
25 means to be employed. The people are less concerned about these than the grand end to be attained. They demand such a reconstruction as shall put an end to the present anarchical state of things in the late rebellious states,—where frightful
30 murders and wholesale massacres are perpetrated in the very presence of Federal soldiers. This horrible business they require shall cease. They want a reconstruction such as will protect loyal men, black and white, in their persons and property; such a one
35 as will cause Northern industry, Northern capital, and Northern civilization to flow into the South, and make a man from New England as much at home in Carolina as elsewhere in the Republic. No Chinese wall can now be tolerated. The South must be
40 opened to the light of law and liberty, and this session of Congress is relied upon to accomplish this important work.

The plain, common sense way of doing this work, as intimated at the beginning, is simply to establish
45 in the South one law, one government, one administration of justice, one condition to the exercise of the elective franchise, for men of all races and colors alike. This great measure is sought as earnestly by loyal white men as by loyal blacks, and
50 is needed alike by both. Let sound political prescience but take the place of an unreasoning prejudice and this will be done.

Men denounce the negro for his prominence in this discussion; but it is no fault of his that in peace
55 as in war, that in conquering Rebel armies as in reconstructing the rebellious States, the right of the negro is the true solution of our national troubles. The stern logic of events, which goes directly to the point, disdaining all concern for the color or features
60 of men, has determined the interests of the country as identical with and inseparable from those of the negro.

The policy that emancipated and armed the negro—now seen to have been wise and proper by
65 the dullest—was not certainly more sternly demanded than is now the policy of enfranchisement. If with the negro was a success in war, and without him a failure, so in peace, it will be found that the nation must fall or flourish with the negro.

70 Fortunately, the Constitution of the United States knows no distinction between citizens on account of color. Neither does it know any difference between a citizen of a state and a citizen of the United States. Citizenship evidently includes all the rights of citizens,
75 whether state or national. If the Constitution knows none, it is clearly no part of the duty of a Republican Congress now to institute one. The mistake of the last session was the attempt to do this very thing, by a renunciation of its power to secure political rights
80 to any class of citizens, with the obvious purpose to allow the rebellious states to disfranchise, if they should see fit, their colored citizens. This unfortunate blunder must now be retrieved, and the emasculated citizenship given to the negro supplanted by that
85 contemplated in the Constitution of the United States, which declares that the citizens of each state shall enjoy all the rights and immunities of citizens of the several states,—so that a legal voter in any state shall be a legal voter in all the states.

1) The main purpose of lines 1-6 ("There ... failed") is to

A) Dismiss rebellion as a terrible act.
B) Redress the institution of slavery.
C) Describe the need for rebellion.
D) Address the need for rebellion as a last resort.

2) Lines 13-19 ("It ... forfeited.") serve mainly to

A) Present the South's disintegration.
B) Pronounce the South's neglected state.
C) Describe the Southern states' ruination.
D) Depict the Southern states' state of dissolution.

3) Over the course of the third paragraph, the focus shifts from

A) A dismissal of responsibility to a new idea.
B) A disclaimer to a call to action.
C) An admittance of lack to a plan of action.
D) A repudiation to a methodology.

4) The central idea of the fourth paragraph is to

A) Define the need for change.
B) Advise on suitable eliminations to be made.
C) Prescribe solutions to transforming the South.
D) Specify actions that might develop the South.

5) What is the function of the seventh paragraph?

A) That the Constitution should not distinguish between state and Federal citizenship.
B) That the Republican Congress blundered in excluding certain people from voting.
C) That voters should be able to vote in all states.
D) That citizenship should be given to all citizens.

Questions 1-5 are based on the following passage adapted from *Flexitarian Diets and Health: A Review of the Evidence-Based Literature,* an article published in Frontiers in Nutrition.

"Flexitarianism" is a neoteric term that has been emerging in the scientific and public sectors recently. Added to the Oxford English Dictionary in 2014, flexitarian is a portmanteau of "flexible" and

5 "vegetarian," referring to an individual who follows a primarily but not strictly vegetarian diet, occasionally eating meat or fish. Despite the global demands for meat, it appears that there are now a growing number of flexitarian consumers who abstain from

10 eating meat regularly.

Most consumers can be grouped into meat consumers, meat avoiders, or meat reducers. The trend toward flexitarian diets (FDs) appears to reflect consumers who are "meat-reducers," eating meat

15 within meals on some but not every day of the week, as with typical "meat-eaters". This definition is most closely in line with that of semi- or demi-vegetarianism. Subsequently, the terms are often used inter-changeably in the literature. For example,

20 in one publication semi-vegetarian diets (SVDs) are defined as those significantly reducing meat intake on at least three days of the week.

The FD seems to recognize the fact that meat is an important source of protein, fat, and micronutrients,

25 yet also considers the ethical sides, such as the need to avoid intensification and improve animal welfare. It also considers evidence that long-term consumption of increasing amounts of red meat and particularly processed meat may increase the risk of

30 mortality, cardiovascular disease, type 2 diabetes, and certain forms of cancer such as colon cancer. Recently, the International Agency for Research on Cancer classified red meat as probably carcinogenic and processed meat carcinogenic to humans.

35 Research from NatCen's British Social Attitudes survey found that 29% of people in Britain have reduced the amount of meat that they ate in the past 12 months. The definition of meat reducers included reductions in all meats except fish. In

40 particular, women (34%) were most likely to reduce their meat intake. Similarly, 39% of 65- to 79-year olds had reduced their red meat intake compared with 19% of 18- to 24-year olds. The report also showed that men (23%) were shifting and reducing

45 their meat intake. Over half (58%) cited health reasons along with saving money, concerns over animal welfare, and food safety.

Six studies focused on SVDs and body weight. Two RCTs looked at the effects of different plant-based

50 diets in relation to weight loss. In one study, authors undertook a 6-month RCT, where overweight adults were allocated to five different plant-based diets. Vegan diets were associated with significantly higher levels of weight loss by the end of the study. A

55 Korean study reported that postmenopausal women maintaining an SVD over 20 years had a significantly lower body weight, body mass index (BMI), and percentage of body fat compared with non-vegetarians (NVs).

60 Cross-sectional data from 71,751 participants taking part in the Adventist Health Study-2 (2002–2007) showed that BMI was highest in NVs (mean 28.7 kg/m^2), slightly lower in SVs (mean 27.4 kg/m^2), and lowest in strict vegetarians (mean 24.0 kg/m^2) .

65 These findings are similar to earlier trends (2002–2006 analysis) showing that mean BMI was lowest in vegans (23.6 kg/m^2) and incrementally higher in lacto-ovo vegetarians (LOVs) (25.7 kg/m^2), pesco-vegetarians (PVs) (26.3 kg/m^2), SVs (27.3 kg/m^2), and

70 NVs (28.8 kg/m^2) . Cross-sectional research on 9,113 young Australian women (22–27 years) identified that SVs had a lower BMI and tended to exercise more than NVs.

The trend of flexitarianism does not appear to be

75 subsiding. This review provides a first line of evidence that FDs may have emerging health benefits in relation to weight loss, metabolic health, and diabetes prevention. While most flexitarians presently seem to be female, there is a clear need to

80 communicate the potential health benefits of these diets to males. As not everyone and in particular men might not want to exclude meat altogether, FDs offer a path that includes their dietary preferences yet could improve public health outcomes.

1) The first paragraph serves mainly to

A) Describe who is a flexitarian.
B) Illustrate a new form of lifestyle.
C) Define what a flexitarian is.
D) Correct a misnomer.

2) The primary purpose of lines 16-18 ("This... vegetarianism") is to

A) Associate similar terms.
B) Differentiate between two root words and their usage to a new term.
C) Define a word.
D) Distinguish a difference.

3) The primary function of the third paragraph is to

A) Give credence to flexitarianism.
B) Purport long term negative effects of a meat-based diet.
C) Acknowledge certain benefits and relate detriments.
D) Claim diseases come from meat-based diets.

4) The primary function of the fourth and sixth paragraphs is to

A) Provide statistics on the reduction of meat consumption and the effects on the weight of various other eaters.
B) Prove meat intake and Body Mass Index are interrelated.
C) Present data that shows people meat eaters are decreasing and that non-meat eaters are affected in various ways.
D) Give facts that contradict each other pertaining to flexitarianism.

5) The central idea of the passage is that

A) Flexitarianism is an eating lifestyle that has positive effects.
B) Flexitarianism is a fad diet.
C) Flexitarianism is a healthy way to eat which can cure diseases.
D) Flexitarianism is a lifestyle choice which is growing but is unsustainable.

Questions 1-5 are based on the following passage adapted from *The Red Badge of Courage* by Stephen Crane.

The cold passed reluctantly from the earth, and the retiring fogs revealed an army stretched out on the hills, resting. As the landscape changed from brown to green, the army awakened and began to
5 tremble with eagerness at the noise of rumors. It cast its eyes upon the roads, which were growing from long troughs of liquid mud to proper thoroughfares. A river, amber-tinted in the shadow of its banks, purled at the army's feet; and at night,
10 when the stream had become of a sorrowful blackness, one could see across it the red, eyelike gleam of hostile camp-fires set in the low brows of distant hills.

Once a certain tall soldier developed virtues and
15 went resolutely to wash a shirt. He came flying back from a brook waving his garment bannerlike. He was swelled with a tale he had heard from a reliable friend, who had heard it from a truthful cavalryman, who had heard it from his trustworthy brother, one
20 of the orderlies at division headquarters. He adopted the important air of a herald in red and gold. "We're goin' t' move t'morrah--sure," he said pompously to a group in the company street. "We're goin' 'way up the river, cut across, an' come around in behint 'em."

25 To his attentive audience, he drew a loud and elaborate plan of a very brilliant campaign. When he had finished, the blue clothed men scattered into small arguing groups between the rows of squat brown huts. A negro teamster who had been dancing
30 upon a cracker box with the hilarious encouragement of two-score soldiers was deserted. He sat mournfully down. Smoke drifted lazily from a multitude of quaint chimneys.

"It's a lie! that's all it is--a thunderin' lie!" said
35 another private loudly. His smooth face was flushed, and his hands were thrust sulkily into his trouser's pockets. He took the matter as an affront to him. "I don't believe the derned old army's ever going to move. We're set. I've got ready to move eight times
40 in the last two weeks, and we ain't moved yet." The tall soldier felt called upon to defend the truth of a rumor he himself had introduced. He and the loud one came near to fighting over it.

A corporal began to swear before the assemblage.
45 He had just put a costly board floor in his house, he said. During the early spring, he had refrained from adding extensively to the comfort of his environment because he had felt that the army might start on the march at any moment. Of late, however, he had
50 been impressed that they were in a sort of eternal camp.

Many of the men engaged in a spirited debate. One outlined in a peculiarly lucid manner all the plans of the commanding general. He was opposed by men
55 who advocated that there were other plans of campaign. They clamored at each other, numbers making futile bids for the popular attention. Meanwhile, the soldier who had fetched the rumor bustled about with much importance. He was
60 continually assailed by questions.

"What's up, Jim?"

"Th'army's goin' t' move."

"Ah, what yeh talkin' about? How yeh know it is?"

"Well, yeh kin b'lieve me er not, jest as yeh like. I
65 don't care a hang."

There was much food for thought in the manner in which he replied. He came near to convincing them by disdaining to produce proofs. They grew much excited over it.

70 There was a youthful private who listened with eager ears to the words of the tall soldier and to the varied comments of his comrades. After receiving a fill of discussions concerning marches and attacks, he went to his hut and crawled through an intricate hole that
75 served it as a door. He wished to be alone with some new thoughts that had lately come to him.

The youth was in a little trance of astonishment. So they were at last going to fight. On the morrow,
80 perhaps, there would be a battle, and he would be in it. For a time, he was obliged to labor to make himself believe. He could not accept with assurance an omen that he was about to mingle in one of those great affairs of the earth.

1) The main purpose of the passage is to

A) Illustrate soldiers' thoughts and actions in war.
B) Give an in-depth view of a soldier's mind at war.
C) Describe soldiers' reactions to going to battle.
D) Show the conflict between soldiers in an army's camp.

2) The first paragraph serves mainly to

A) Foreshadow the setting of the war.
B) Establish the setting of the story.
C) Provide background information for later in the story.
D) Illustrate an area of focus for the reader to relate to the events in the story.

3) The central problem of the fourth paragraph is

A) A soldier's fear of going to war.
B) Two soldiers disagree with each other on the actions of a superior.
C) Disregard for another soldier's opinion.
D) Disbelief in a rumor.

4) The first sentence of the fifth paragraph serves to
A) Prove the veracity of previous statements.
B) Inspire the morale of his soldiers.
C) Declare allegiance to the people assembled.
D) Show disapproval for presumed events.

5) The primary function of the ninth and tenth paragraphs is to

A) Summarize the feelings of the soldiers.
B) Reveal the fears of a soldier.
C) Elucidate on the ruminations of a soldier.
D) Construe the intentions of a soldier.

Questions 1-5 are based on the following passage adapted from *The Poor Man's Garden from Social Notes, London, England.*

Among the chief of the many improvements which this our dingy metropolis has received within the last few years, must be classed the attention given to flowers and window gardens. The very rich
5 have their conservatories and plantations, the well-to-do in London their greenhouse and their parterre, the humbler lovers of all green things their fern case and flower stands; but the dwellers in the one back room, the weary city clerk with his limited salary, his
10 many mouths to feed, and his circumscribed house room, have only their window garden—their long wooden box, enriched it may be with gaudy tiles—wherein to plant their childhood's favorites and keep the color of God's carpet green in their memories.

15 Flowers and music make the poetry of life, and the more the toilers in this city of brick and mortar are made familiar with them, the better for their mental and moral health. This conviction has spread rapidly during the last few years, the rich having set the
20 example by festooning their townhouses with hardy climbers, while their balconies are filled in summer with flowers.

The subtle influence of flowers on mankind is so thoroughly admitted, that it seems as though the
25 remembrance of the 'garden the Lord planted' has never died out of the perception of the human race; the love and cultivation of plants has always had an elevating tendency—a drawing near to those far off days of innocence when the trees and flowers and
30 song of the wild bird were man's delight, as he 'walked with God.'

The Dean of Westminster, other dignitaries of the Church, highborn ladies, and people of wealth and leisure, have done much lately towards fostering this
35 growing feeling among all classes by giving prizes for the best plants grown in dingy back yards and smoky garret rooms; and it is as astonishing as it is touching to find how, like a human being, the little plant adapts itself to its surroundings, and throws out its
40 beauty and fragrance in return for a little patience and tender care.

Annual exhibitions of workmen's flowers take place patronized by the highest in the land; in all directions efforts are being made to spread the
45 growing taste, and, above all, to give the toiling man and woman a home interest, a something to tend and watch, which is nature's only safeguard against selfishness.

After those plant shows, where children exhibit, if
50 the little window gardeners were encouraged to give their prize blossoms to the old and sick of their acquaintance, a feeling of kindliness and generosity in the young would be sown that would bear the fruits of charity hereafter.

55 I believe that flower sermons are given now and then by those good clergymen who have a special interest in the young. Each child brings a flower, and he tells them all he knows of the flowers that Christ hallowed by name; so God's living gems become
60 sacred in the child's memory, not to be plucked and cast away at a moment's whim.

The culture of plants in our crowded back slums and alleys would be most beneficial to the health, plants living on certain gases we exhale; and it seems
65 impossible to conceive that a lover of flowers can be quite hardened in heart—there must be a soft spot where the arrow of religious conviction may penetrate if aimed by a skillful archer. The ministers of religion might do worse than foster window
70 gardening in districts where they visit.

Many have heard of the 'Flower Mission.' Little bunches of flowers are made up by ladies' fingers and sent to hospitals, and to many, a leaflet is attached on which a short sentence of scripture is
75 written. I am told that the happiest results have ensued. Men and women whom the word of chaplain failed to soften, at the sight of a flower have 'given in' and wept! Days of past innocence and happiness crowded into their memories by the
80 ministration of a homely wallflower.

To those with gardens full of flowering shrubs and conservatories radiant with scented beauty, to the more homely garden lover with borders full of wallflowers and lily of the valley, with walls
85 burdened with monthly roses and honeysuckle, I say, give of your abundance to the sick in mind and body. Once a week during the bounteous flower season send to some hospital, workhouse, or infirmary a hamper of God's living gems. Be a member of the
90 'Flower Mission' in all its branches, in the window, the sick room, and to the aged pauper.

1) The first paragraph serves mainly to

A) Explain the emergence of window gardens.
B) Illustrate the narrator's views on gardening.
C) Describe the different types of social gardening.
D) Elaborate on the rich's taste in gardening.

2) What function does the second paragraph serve in the passage as a whole?

A) An explanation of the advantages of window gardens and types.
B) A description of the benefits of window gardening and its origins.
C) An illustration of the importance of window gardens and their uses.
D) A characterization of window gardens and the people who influenced their start.

3) The central idea of the fourth paragraph is that

A) Social events have been established to promote window gardening.
B) High society competes with each other in window gardening contests.
C) Contests for window gardening have been established.
D) People have begun gardening and plants change according to their environments.

4) The primary function of the seventh and eighth paragraphs is to

A) Show the effects of flowers on children.
B) Illustrate the religious value of flowers.
C) Describe the benefit of flowers on the youth and the inner-city residents.
D) Validate the cultural importance of flowers.

5) The last paragraph serves mainly as

A) A suggestion to grow better.
B) An acknowledgement of appreciation.
C) A call to action.
D) A plea to do more to grow the gardening movement.

Questions 1-5 are based on the following passage adapted from *What Is Marine Biodiversity? Towards Common Concepts and Their Implications for Assessing Biodiversity Status,* an article published in Frontiers in Marine Science Journal.

The term "biodiversity", first used almost three decades ago as a derivative of "biological diversity", today is one of the most often cited terms in both ecological research and environmental management 5 and conservation. However, its precise definition and our understanding of the concept varies widely both between and within disciplines. Biodiversity is recognized to encompass "the variability among living organisms from all sources including, among 10 other things, terrestrial, marine, and other aquatic ecosystems and the ecological complexes of which they are part; this includes diversity within species, between species and of ecosystems."

The elements of biodiversity are fundamental 15 properties of an ecosystem, and, in the marine realm, these encompass all life forms, including the environments they inhabit, and at scales from genes and species to ecosystems. Biodiversity can be described as an abstract aggregated property of 20 those ecosystem components and can relate to the structure or function of the community where structure relates to the system at one time whereas functioning relates to rate processes.

The structural aspect is represented by the various 25 marine life-forms, ranging from the smallest prokaryote to the largest mammal, and inhabiting some of the most extreme environments. These species exhibit a diversity that probably exceeds that found in terrestrial environments. The functional 30 aspect is represented by the relationships among and between these marine organisms and the environments they inhabit and is defined in terms of rates of ecological processes; most notably they include physiological processes, predator-prey 35 relationships, trophic webs, competition, and resource partitioning. These functions vary on both temporal and spatial scales and include some of the most important ecosystem services, including oxygen provisioning, CO_2 sequestration, and re- 40 mineralization of nutrients. Both structural and functional elements contributing to biodiversity play a fundamental role in maintaining and defining healthy marine systems.

In essence, the marine ecosystem is comprised of 45 three interlinked processes. Firstly, the physico-chemical system creates a set of fundamental niches which then are colonized by organisms according to their environmental tolerances—these may be termed environment-biology relationships. Secondly, 50 the organisms interact with each other in, for example, predator-prey interactions, competition, recruitment, feeding, and mutualism—these are biology-biology relationships. Thirdly, the resulting ecology has the ability to complete the cycle with 55 feedback loops and modify the physico-chemical system through bioturbation, space or material removal or change, bio-engineering, for example; these may be termed biology-environment relationships. Anthropogenic influences then perturb 60 the systems.

Human activities produce a range of pressures on marine systems, some of which may lead to irreversible changes. This may have immediate consequences for patterns of biodiversity and 65 consequently for the critical ecosystem services they provide. Those ecosystem services can be grouped into provisioning, regulating, supporting and cultural ones which, after adding human complementary assets, in turn lead to societal benefits.

70 In this context, the European Marine Strategy Framework Directive (MSFD) requires Member States to achieve Good Environmental Status (GES). The directive comprises 11 qualitative descriptors of GES, of which biological diversity is the first, but 75 most if not all of the others can be considered to refer to some part of biodiversity in its broad sense. In order to know whether the goal of GES has been achieved, an assessment needs to be performed that measures the current environmental status, hence 80 this involves quantifying the abstract ecosystem feature biodiversity. For this, the European Commission has defined a number of GES criteria and indicators that represent and quantify various aspects of environmental status and biodiversity. 85 The available indicators in Europe, for the MSFD implementation, have been recently collated, and a method to select the most adequate has been proposed. Then, some of them have been used in assessing the environmental status across regional 90 seas.

1) The passage primarily serves to

A) Discuss how biodiversity is important to the environment.
B) Define biodiversity and human assessments of it.
C) Explain the different biodiverse environments and man's tainting of them.
D) Describe several biomes and human engagement with them.

2) The primary purpose of lines 7-12 ("Biodiversity ... part") is to

A) Describe the general composition of biodiversity with meticulous details.
B) Explain the extent of what biodiversity encompasses, includes, and excludes.
C) Clarify the meaning of biodiversity by explaining all the aspects of it.
D) Define biodiversity and give basic examples.

3) The central idea of the third paragraph is

A) The structural and functional aspects of marine environments.
B) The different processes that take place to produce biodiversity in marine environments.
C) The differences in biodiversity between marine environments and terrestrial environments.
D) Maintaining and defining healthy marine systems.

4) Over the course of the passage, the focus shifts from

A) An explanation of different biodiverse environments to human interaction with them.
B) A description of biodiversity to human activities related to it.
C) Different examples of biodiversity to changes in governmental understanding of them.
 D) Challenges to biodiversity to numerous solutions to solving them.

5) The second to the last sentence of the passage mainly serves to

A) Report progress to setting up an assessment system.
B) Identify processes needed to be enacted to solve man-made biodiversity problems.
C) Develop a protocol to assess environments.
D) Introduce a new system to study biodiversity.

Questions 1-5 are based on the following passage adapted from *Mdm. de Staël Famous Women Series* by Bella Duffy.

"My dear friend having the same tastes as myself, would certainly wish always for my chair, and, like his little daughter, would beat me to make me give it up to him to keep peace between our hearts, I send
5 a chair for him also. The two are of suitable height and their lightness renders them easy to carry. They are made of the simplest material, and were bought at the sale of Philemon and Baucis."

Thus, wrote Madame Geoffrin to Madame Necker
10 when the intimacy between them had reached such a pitch as to warrant the introduction into the Necker salons of the only sort of chair in which the little old lady cared to sit.

The "dear friend" was Madame Necker, and the
15 "little daughter" of the house must then have been about four or five years old, for it was in the very year of her birth that Madame Geoffrin took her celebrated journey to Poland, and it was some little time after her return that she became intimate with
20 Germaine Necker's parents.

They were still in the Rue de Cléry in Paris. Mister Necker's elevation to the Contrôle Général was in the future and had probably not been foreseen; it is possible that even the *Éloge de Colbert*, which
25 betrayed his desire for power, had not yet appeared; nevertheless, he was already a great man. His controversy with the Abbé Morellet, on the subject of the East India Company, had brought him very much into notice; and, although his arguments in
30 favor of that monopoly had not saved it from extinction, they had caused his name to be in everybody's mouth.

His position as Minister for the Republic of Geneva gave him the entry to the Court of Versailles and
35 brought him into contact with illustrious personages, who otherwise might have disdained a mere wealthy foreigner, neither a noble nor a Catholic. His well-filled purse completed his popularity, for it was not seldom at the service of abject place hunters and
40 needy literati. Moreover, he had been fortunate in his choice of a wife.

But Madame Necker, besides being young, rich and handsome, was bitten with the prevailing craze for literature, could listen unweariedly for hours to
45 the most labored *portraits* and *éloges*, and, although herself the purest and most austere of women,
would open her salon to any reprobate, provided only he were witty.

Madame Necker, first known to us as Suzanne
50 Curchod, was the daughter of a Swiss pastor, and saw the light in the Presbytery of Crassier in the Pays de Vaud. The simple white house, with its green shutters, is still to be seen, separated from the road by a little garden planted with fruit trees. The
55 Curchods were an ancient and respectable family whom Madame Necker (it was one of her weaknesses) would fain have proved entitled to patents of nobility. Some Curchods or Curchodis are found mentioned in old chronicles as fighting
60 beneath the banners of Savoy, and it was from these that Madame Necker sought vainly to trace her descent. She held a secret consultation for this cherished object with the Sieur Chérin, genealogist to the King; but his decision disappointed her.
65 Chagrined, but not convinced—for her opinions were not easily shaken—she carried home the precious papers and locked them up without erasing the endorsement, *Titres de noblesse de la famille Curchod*, which she had written with her own hand.

70 Mister Curchod took pains to give his only daughter an unusually thorough and liberal education. She knew Latin and a little Greek, "swept with extreme flounce the circle of the sciences," and was accomplished enough in every way to attract the
75 admiration, very often even the love, of sundry grave and learned personages.

Mixed with her severe charm there must have been some coquetry, for at a very early age she began making conquests among the young ministers
80 who arrived on Sundays at Crassier, ostensibly to assist Mister Curchod in his duties; and a voluminous correspondence, somewhat high flown, as was the fashion of the day, is extant, to prove that Suzanne possessed the art of keeping her numerous admirers
85 simultaneously well in hand. Verses, occasionally slightly Voltairian in tone, were also addressed to her; and later in life, Madame Necker reproached herself for her placid acceptance of the homage thus expressed, and owned that had she understood it
90 better she would have liked it less.

1) The main idea of the passage is that of

A) A husband and wife of high society.
B) Two women belonging to a salon.
C) A woman's current life and her earlier life.
D) The upper class of society in France.

2) The first paragraph serves mainly to

A) Foreshadow the relationship between two children.
B) Compare the temperance of a girl and a boy.
C) Describe an abusive relationship.
D) Establish two friend's interactions.

3) What function does the second paragraph serve in the passage as a whole?

A) It discloses contents of a letter between friends.
B) It describes the preferences of a woman.
C) It establishes the relationship between two people.
D) It introduces two characters.

4) Over the course of the passage, the focus shifts from

A) High society in Paris to a woman's early life.
B) A woman's introduction to her early life.
C) Two women's friendship to their falling out.
D) The interaction of a woman and a couple to the woman's new life.

5) The last paragraph serves mainly as

A) A woman's recollection of her reckless attitude.
B) A woman's regret for her earlier flirtatious ways.
C) The remembrances of a woman's childhood.
D) The reminiscence of a woman's interactions with her father and her contentment with them.

Questions 1-5 are based on the following passage adapted from *Car indoor air pollution - analysis of potential sources published in the Journal of Occupational Medicine and Toxicology*.

Air quality plays an important role in occupational and environmental medicine and many airborne factors negatively influence human health. Air pollution is the emission of toxic elements into the
5 atmosphere by natural or anthropogenic sources. These sources can be further differentiated into either mobile or stationary sources. Anthropogenic air pollution is often summarized as being mainly related to motorized street traffic, especially exhaust
10 gases and tire abrasion. Whereas other sources including the burning of fuels, and larger factory emissions are also very important, public debate usually addresses car emissions.

The World Health Organization (WHO) estimates
15 2.4 million fatalities due to air pollution every year. Since the breathing of polluted air can have severe health effects such as asthma, COPD or increased cardiovascular risks, most countries have strengthened laws to control the air quality and
20 mainly focus on emissions from automobiles.

One general study assessed the exposure to fine airborne particulate matter (PM2.5) in closed vehicles. It was reported that this may be associated with cardiovascular events and mortality in older and
25 cardiac patients. Potential physiologic effects of in-vehicle, roadside, and ambient PM2.5 were investigated in young, healthy, non-smoking, male North Carolina Highway Patrol troopers. Nine troopers (age 23 to 30) were monitored on 4
30 successive days while working a 3 P.M. to midnight shift. Each patrol car was equipped with air-quality monitors. Blood was drawn 14 hours after each shift, and ambulatory monitors recorded the electrocardiogram throughout the shift and until the
35 next morning. Data were analyzed using mixed models. In-vehicle PM2.5 average of 24 µg/m3 was associated with decreased lymphocytes -11% per 10 µg/m3 and increased red blood cell indices 1% mean

corpuscular volume, neutrophils 6%, C-reactive
40 protein 32%, von Willebrand factor 12%, next-morning heartbeat cycle length 6%, next-morning heart rate variability parameters, and ectopic beats throughout the recording 20% . Controlling for potential confounders had little impact on the effect
45 estimates. The associations of these health endpoints with ambient and roadside PM2.5 were smaller and less significant. The observations in these healthy young men suggest that in-vehicle exposure to PM2.5 may cause pathophysiologic
50 changes that involve inflammation, coagulation, and cardiac rhythm.

A second study by Riedecker et al. assessed if the exposure to fine PM2.5 from traffic affects heart-rate variability, thrombosis, and inflammation. This work
55 was a reanalysis and investigated components potentially contributing to such effects in non-smoking healthy male North Carolina highway patrol troopers. The authors studied nine officers four times during their late shift. PM2.5, its elemental
60 composition, and gaseous copollutants were measured inside patrol cars. Components correlating to PM2.5 were compared by Riedecker et al. to cardiac and blood parameters measured 10 and 15 hours, respectively, after each shift. The study
65 demonstrated that components that were associated with health endpoints independently from PM2.5 were calcium, chromium, aldehydes, copper, and sulfur.

The changes that were observed in this reanalysis
70 were consistent with effects reported earlier for PM2.5 from speed-change and from soil . However, the associations of chromium with inflammation markers were not found before for traffic particles. The authors concluded that aldehydes, calcium,
75 copper, sulfur, and chromium or compounds containing these elements seem to directly contribute to the inflammatory and cardiac response to PM2.5 from traffic in the investigated patrol troopers.

*µg/m3 -microgram per cubic meter

1) The central claim of the passage is that

A) Automobiles emit pollution.
B) Police are highly susceptible to in-vehicle pollution due to lengthy shift.
C) The interior of cars contain auto emissions that can be harmful.
 D) Air-quality is affected by pollution that contains numerous elemental components.

2) The main purpose of lines 1-3 ("Air ... health") is to

A) Illustrate the importance of air-quality.
B) Define changes of air quality.
C) Elaborate on the negative impacts of airborne factors.
D) Describe what air quality affects.

3) The first paragraph serves mainly to

A) Define man-made air pollution.
B) Illustrate the problems of pollution.
C) Note about man-made pollution.
D) Present a man-made problem.

4) The primary function of the third and fourth paragraphs is to

A) Focus on the negative effects of pollution particles on test subjects and the components.
B) Describe the ways pollution affects police officers and why.
C) Report on the effects pollution has on specific parts of the body and how to reduce those effects.
D) Introduce a need for further pollution studies to analyze its effects and reverse the effects.

5) The last paragraph serves mainly to

A) Confirm a finding and update how the components of pollution affect the body.
B) Conclude the findings and restate the effects on the body.
C) Summarize the findings of a study.
D) Show how pollution has a negative effect on the body.

Questions 1-5 are based on the following passage adapted from *The Spell of the Rockies* by Enos A. Mills

Scattered flakes of ashes were falling when a herd of elk led the exodus of wild folk from the fire doomed forest. They came stringing out of the woods into the open, with both old and young going
5 forward without confusion and as though headed for a definite place or pasture. They splashed through a pond without stopping and continued their way up the river. There was no show of fear, no suggestion of retreat. They never looked back. Deer straggled
10 out singly and in groups. It was plain that all were fleeing from danger, all were excitedly trying to get out of the way of something; and they did not appear to know where they were going. Apparently they gave more troubled attention to the roaring,
15 the breath, and the movements of that fiery, mysterious monster than to the seeking of a place of permanent safety. In the grassy open, into which the smoke was beginning to drift and hang, the deer scattered and lingered. At each roar of the fire, they
20 turned hither and thither excitedly to look and listen. A flock of mountain sheep, in a long, narrow, closely pressed rank and led by an alert, aggressive bighorn, presented a fine appearance as it raced into the open. The admirable directness of these wild animals
25 put them out of the category occupied by tame, "silly sheep." Without slackening pace, they swept across the grassy valley in a straight line and vanished in the wooded slope beyond. Now and then a coyote appeared from somewhere and stopped for a time in
30 the open among the deer; all these wise little wolves were a trifle nervous, but each had himself well in hand. Glimpses were had of two stealthy mountain lions, now leaping, now creeping, now swiftly fleeing.

Bears were the most matter-of-fact fellows in the
35 exodus. Each loitered in the grass and occasionally looked toward the oncoming danger. Their actions showed curiosity and anger, but not alarm. Each duly took notice of the surrounding animals, and one old grizzly even struck viciously at a snarling coyote. Two
40 black bear cubs, true to their nature, had a merry romp. Even these serious conditions could not make them solemn. Each tried to prevent the other from climbing a tree that stood alone in the open; around this tree they clinched, cuffed, and rolled about so
45 merrily that the frightened wild folks were attracted and momentarily forgot their fears.

With subdued and ever-varying roar, the fire steadily advanced. It constantly threw off an upcurling, unbroken cloud of heavy smoke that hid
50 the flames from view. Now and then a whirl of wind brought a shower of sparks together with bits of burning bark out over the open valley.

Just as the flames were reaching the margin of the forest a great bank of black smoke curled forward
55 and then appeared to fall into the grassy open. I had just a glimpse of a few fleeing animals, then all became hot, fiery, and dark. Red flames darted through swirling black smoke. It was stifling. M; into a beaver pond, I lowered my own sizzling
60 temperature and that of my smoking clothes. The air was too hot and black for breathing; so I fled, floundering through the water, down Grand River.

A quarter of a mile took me beyond the danger-line and gave me fresh air. Here the smoke ceased to
65 settle to the earth but extended in a light upcurling stratum a few yards above it. Through this smoke, the sunlight came so changed that everything around me was magically covered with a canvas of sepia or rich golden brown. I touched the burned spots on
70 hands and face with real, though raw, balsam and then plunged into the burned over district to explore the extensive ruins of the fire.

As known to me and other outdoorsmen, a prairie fire commonly consumes everything to the earth line
75 and leaves behind it only a black field. The fire burns away the smaller limbs and the foliage, leaving the tree standing all blackened and bristling. This fire, as I could see about me, consumed the litter carpet on the forest floor and the mossy covering of the rocks;
80 it ate the underbrush, devoured the foliage, charred and burned the limbs, and blackened the trunks. Behind was a dead forest in a desolate field, a territory with millions of bristling, mutilated trees, a forest ruin impressively picturesque and pathetic.

85 When I entered the burn that afternoon, the fallen trees that the fire had found were in ashes, the trees just killed were smoking, while the standing dead trees were just beginning to burn freely. That night, these scattered beacons strangely burned among the
90 multitudinous dead. Close to my camp, all through that night several of these fire columns showered sparks like a fountain, glowed and occasionally lighted up the scene with flaming torches. Weird and strange in the night were the groups of silhouetted
95 figures in a shadow-dance between me and the flickering, heroic torches.

1) The main purpose of the passage is to

A) Illustrate the personal experience of the narrator.
B) Describe the scenes of a conflagration.
C) Convey the narrator's concern about forest fires.
D) Explain the effects of a forest fire.

2) What function does the first paragraph serve in the passage as?

A) An explanation of a forest fire's destructive path.
B) An account of animals' flight from a danger.
C) A recount of the narrator's terrifying experience.
D) A depiction of animals in their natural habitat.

3) The last sentence of the sixth paragraph mainly serves to

A) Show the aftermath of a natural disaster.
B) Depict the devastation of a forest fire.
C) Provide examples of disasters in forests.
D) Warn of the dangers caused by forest fires.

4) Over the course of the passage, the focus shifts from

A) An adventure to a tragedy.
B) A natural disaster to a heroic act.
C) A flight to personal observations.
D) A disturbance to a conclusion.

5) The main idea of the final paragraph is that of

A) An untimely event.
B) An eerie occurrence.
C) A strange conclusion.
D) A morbid observation.

Questions 1-5 are based on the following passage adapted from *The principal sources of William James' idea of habit,* an article published in Frontiers Journal.

James consecrated the fourth chapter of his *Principles of Psychology* to the explanation of the idea of habit, for "when we look at living creatures from an outward point of view, one of the first things
5 that strike us is that they are bundles of habits. In wild animals, the usual round of daily behavior seems a necessity implanted at birth; in animals domesticated, and especially in man, it seems, to a great extent, to be the result of education. The
10 habits to which there is an innate tendency are called instincts; some of those due to education would by most persons be called acts of reason"

The first relevant idea exposed by William James concerns the importance of plasticity in the
15 development of all organic forms. Habit, enabled by this universally manifested–though in growing degrees- plasticity, is the biological correlate of the idea of natural law in the inanimate universe. In his own words, "the laws of Nature are nothing but the
20 immutable habits which the different elementary sorts of matter follow in their actions and reactions upon each other." Habit as the organic transposition of a natural law constitutes one of the guiding principles of James approach to this category. Its
25 sources can be found in several authors. One of them is Léon Dumont, a French psychologist whose essay *De l'Habitude* is quoted by James. In this text, Dumont, following August Comte, had written that the idea of habit expresses, better than anyone else,
30 the notion of a gradual acquisition of new faculties. According to him, the evolutionary perspective finds a good ally in the idea of habit, for it contains the progressive perfectibility of all beings, including man. In his studies of habit, sensibility and evolution,
35 Dumont understood habit in analogy with the laws of inanimate nature.

A second major source of influence on James is the work of William Benjamin Carpenter, an English physician and physiologist who had done extensive
40 work on comparative neurology. He spoke in terms of "adaptive unconscious" in which there are resonances of Hermann von Helmholtz's conception of thought and perception as drawing unconscious hypotheses and inferring probabilistic accounts
45 about the surrounding environment. According to this theory, thought and perception would operate, to a large extent, without awareness, and we would remain unconscious about a substantial body of mental phenomena which we consider rooted in the
50 deepest powers of consciousness. As in the case of Dumont, in Carpenter, there is a clear influence of Darwin's theory of evolution.

James conceived of a habit as the fruit of the exceptional plasticity of organic life, whose versatility
55 would have played a significant role in favoring the adaption to different environment, needs, and challenges. But beyond the biological and evolutionary basis of habits, James wanted to unfold the formation of this kind of automatized behavior.
60 To answer this question, he found inspiration in the work of English utilitarian philosophers like Alexander Bain and John Stuart Mill. Bain, a Scottish psychologist and a leading figure of empiricism, had like Mill (whom he revered) endorsed an
65 associationist approach to the acquisition of new behaviors.

James went a step further and delineated a refined view of habits in which the ideas of plasticity, automatization, and association were carefully
70 bounded. For him, a habit corresponded to a general form of discharge that helped concentrate energies on unpredicted challenges. As he wrote, following Carpenter's idea that our nervous system grows to the modes in which it has been exercised, "habit
75 simplifies the movements required to achieve a given result, makes them more accurate and diminishes fatigue". In James' view, this is perhaps the most remarkable feature of a habit: it diminishes the conscious attention with which our acts are
80 performed. The precedents to this idea can be found in the work of the French spiritualist philosopher François-Pierre Maine de Biran According to James, the ability to act without the concourse of will has clear advantages. In a habitual action, mere
85 sensation suffices for eliciting muscular movements, so that the upper regions of the brain and mind are set "comparatively free," unless they go wrong and they immediately call our attention. This liberation shows extremely beneficial for displaying a larger
90 array of actions.

1) During the course of the first paragraph, the narrator's focus shifts from

 A) General habits of living things to their specific habits.
B) An explanation of habits to citing specific habits.
C) A description of certain habits to habits of education.
D) The difference in habits based on instinct and education.

2) The primary purpose of lines 31-33 ("According... man") is to
A) Show that evolution and habit can be progressive.
B) Prove that evolution and habit help beings to gradually work towards perfection.
C) Dismiss the idea that evolution and habit assist organisms.
D) Relate the qualities of evolution and habit.

3) The third paragraph serves mainly to

A) Cite a second major source of influence on James.
B) Explain the use of consciousness in habit-forming processes.
C) Contrast the idea that the natural law of matter is an action and reaction by stating that there is a profound mental root to habit.
D) Describe a mental phenomenon caused by awareness of one's circumstances.

4) The central question of paragraph four is

A) How does evolution and habit effect behavior?
B) Why are organisms' actions reflexive?
C) How do wild and domesticated animals develop habits?
D) Why did plasticity play such a main part in evolution?

5) The primary purpose of lines 78-80 ("it ... performed") is to show
A) That habit needs little concentration to develop
B) That an automatized being need not focus to develop habitual skills.
C) That conscious attention is needed on performed acts.
D) That beings which act with habit focus less on tasks.

Questions 1-5 are based on the following passage adapted from *Green Infrastructure Opportunities that Arise During Municipal Operations* at https://www.epa.gov/

Green infrastructure uses natural processes to improve water quality and manage water quantity by restoring the hydrologic function of the urban landscape, managing stormwater at its source, and
5   reducing the need for additional gray infrastructure in many instances. These practices are designed to restore the hydrologic function of the urban landscape, managing stormwater at its source and reducing or eliminating the need for gray
10 infrastructure. An important objective of green infrastructure is to reduce stormwater volume, which improves water quality by reducing pollutant loads, stream bank erosion, and sedimentation. When green infrastructure is employed as part of a
15 larger-scale stormwater management system, it reduces the volume of stormwater that requires conveyance and treatment through conventional means, such as detention ponds. Green infrastructure practices can be integrated into
20 existing features of the built environment, including streets, parking lots, and landscaped areas.

Green infrastructure practices can be a viable option for managing stormwater in highly urbanized and infill situations where development density is
25 desired and offsite mitigation is not a preferred alternative.

This document provides approaches local government officials and municipal program managers in small to midsize communities can use to
30 incorporate green infrastructure components into work they are doing in public spaces. The guide demonstrates ways in which projects can be modified relatively easily and at a low cost recognizing that municipal resources can be limited.
35

Implementing projects in public spaces can showcase the aesthetic appeal of green infrastructure practices and provide a visual demonstration of how they can function. This real-
40 life context will also allow residents, businesses, and local governments to experience additional benefits and values of many green infrastructure practices— more walkable streets, traffic calming, green public spaces, shade, and enhanced foot traffic in retail
45 areas. Municipal managers can then use the

experience gained from the design, installation and maintenance green infrastructure projects to help tailor regulations and incentive programs and make green infrastructure easier to implement in the
50 future.

These highlighted examples and case studies show how integrating green infrastructure methods can enhance retrofits and maintenance projects and also provide multiple community benefits. Local
55 governments are in a unique leadership position to further green infrastructure within their communities. The U.S. Environmental Protection Agency (EPA) hopes that by using this guide, localities can begin to institutionalize the use of
60 green infrastructure in their municipal operations. Local agencies are often tasked with retrofitting a property or installing or replacing stormwater and drainage infrastructure. Overall, green infrastructure has been shown to be more cost-effective when
65 compared with traditional gray infrastructure approaches, and green infrastructure offers numerous ancillary benefits. The visible, above- ground and accessible qualities of green infrastructure, as opposed to gray infrastructure,
70 provide other benefits, including, improving air and water quality, improving quality of life, and offering public education opportunities.

Though green infrastructure can potentially have higher installation costs in redevelopment and
75 retrofit settings, this is not always the case due to the site-specific opportunities and constraints on many infrastructure projects. Since gray infrastructure retrofits can also be costly, green infrastructure can be integrated into already planned
80 infrastructure improvement projects to help mitigate demolition and disposal costs.

From a life cycle perspective, it is important to compare the long-term maintenance and replacement costs associated with green and gray
85 infrastructure. The vegetation characteristic of many green infrastructure practices becomes enhanced as it grows over time, whereas gray infrastructure's engineered materials only deteriorate over the long term. The maintenance required for green
90 infrastructure practices typically does not require heavy equipment, whereas maintaining gray infrastructure's pipes, forebays, basins, and embankments can be more costly.

1) The passage primarily serves to

A) Explain how natural processes improve water quality.
B) Define the meaning and specifics of implementing green infrastructure.
C) Determine the value of green infrastructure for cities.
D) Provide a basic understanding of green infrastructure and its benefits.

2) The main purpose of the opening sentence of the passage is to

A) State the purpose of green infrastructure.
B) Inform the reader of the interaction between green infrastructure and hydrologic function.
C) Describe the development of green infrastructure.
D) Express the author's opinion on green infrastructure.

3) The main purpose of the third paragraph is to

A) Inform the reader of the overall purpose of green infrastructure.
B) Provide details of the EPA's mission.
C) Explain the purpose of the passage.
D) Instruct civil servants on how to implement green infrastructure.

4) The primary purpose of lines 36-39 ("Implementing ... function") is to

A) Agree with an action.
B) Describe benefits.
C) Persuade the reader .
D) Disclose disadvantages.

5) The final paragraph serves to

A) Compare two types of infrastructure.
B) Contrast two types of infrastructure.
C) Compare and contrast grey and green infrastructure.
D) Compare and contrast benefits versus disadvantages of green infrastructure.

Questions 1-5 are based on the following passage adapted from *Silas Marner* by George Eliot

When the sunshine grew strong and lasting, so that the buttercups were thick in the meadows, Silas might be seen in the sunny midday, or in the late afternoon when the shadows were lengthening
5 under the hedgerows, strolling out with uncovered head to carry Eppie beyond the Stone-pits to where the flowers grew. Travel they did till they reached some favorite bank where Silas could sit down, while Eppie toddled to pluck the flowers and make
10 remarks to the winged things that murmured happily above the bright petals, calling "Dad-dad's" attention continually by bringing him the flowers. Then she would turn her ear to some sudden bird-note, and Silas learned to please her by making signs of hushed
15 stillness, that they might listen for the note to come again: so that when it came, she set up her small back and laughed with gurgling triumph. Sitting on the banks in this way, Silas began to take refuge in Eppie's little world, that lay lightly on his enfeebled
20 spirit.

As the child's mind was growing into knowledge, his mind was growing into memory: as her life unfolded, his soul, long stupefied in a cold, narrow prison, was unfolding too and trembling gradually
25 into full consciousness.

The tones that stirred Silas's heart grew articulate, and called for more distinct answers; shapes and sounds grew clearer for Eppie's eyes and ears, and there was more that "Dad-dad" was
30 imperatively required to notice and account for. Also, by the time Eppie was three years old, she developed a fine capacity for mischief, and for devising ingenious ways of being troublesome, which found much exercise, not only for Silas's patience but for
35 his watchfulness and penetration. Sorely was poor Silas puzzled on such occasions by the incompatible demands of love. Dolly Winthrop told him that punishment was good for Eppie, and that, as for rearing a child without making it tingle a little in soft
40 and safe places now and then, it was not to be done.

"To be sure, there's another thing you might do, Master Marner," added Dolly, meditatively: "you might shut her up once i' the coal-hole. That was what I did wi' Aaron; for I was that silly wi' the

45 youngest lad, as I could never bear to smack him. Not as I could find i' my heart to let him stay i' the coal-hole more nor a minute, but it was enough to colly him all over, so as he must be new washed and dressed, and it was as good as a rod to him—that
50 was. But I put it upo' your conscience, Master Marner, as there's one of 'em you must choose—ayther smacking or the coal-hole—else she'll get so masterful, there'll be no holding her."

Silas was impressed with the melancholy truth
55 of this last remark; but his force of mind failed before the only two penal methods open to him, not only because it was painful to him to hurt Eppie, but because he trembled at a moment's contention with her, lest she should love him the less for it. It was
60 clear that Eppie, with her short toddling steps, must lead father Silas a pretty dance on any fine morning when circumstances favored mischief.

For example, he had wisely chosen a broad strip of linen as a means of fastening her to his loom
65 when he was busy: it made a broad belt round her waist, and was long enough to allow of her reaching the truckle-bed and sitting down on it, but not long enough for her to attempt any dangerous climbing. One bright summer's morning, Silas had been more
70 engrossed than usual in "setting up" a new piece of work, an occasion on which his scissors were in requisition. These scissors, owing to an especial warning of Dolly's, had been kept carefully out of Eppie's reach; but the click of them had had a
75 peculiar attraction for her ear, and watching the results of that click, she had derived the philosophic lesson that the same cause would produce the same effect. Silas had seated himself in his loom, and the noise of weaving had begun; but he had left his
80 scissors on a ledge which Eppie's arm was long enough to reach; and now, like a small mouse, watching her opportunity, she stole quietly from her corner, secured the scissors, and toddled to the bed again, setting up her back as a mode of concealing
85 the fact. She had a distinct intention as to the use of the scissors; and having cut the linen strip in a jagged but effectual manner, in two moments, she had run out at the open door where the sunshine was inviting her, while poor Silas believed her to be a
90 better child than usual. It was not until he happened to need his scissors that the terrible fact burst upon him: Eppie had run out by herself.

1) Which choice best summarizes the passage?

A) A character develops platonic feelings for another.
B) A character is faced with the challenges of raising his daughter.
C) A mischievous daughter outwits her feeble-minded father.
 D) An ambivalent father considers disciplinary actions for his daughter.

2) What function do lines 18-20 (Silas...spirit) serve in the first paragraph?

A) They depict a man relaxing in the simplicity of being with his daughter playfulness.
B) They illustrate his susceptibility to his daughter's charms.
C) They give an overview of his life through daily activities.
D) They describe a man's ability to envelop himself in fictional fantasies.

3) During the course of the second paragraph, the narrator's focus shifts from

A) One character's growth to another's recollection of broken promises.
B) One character's growth to another's reflection on aging.
C) One character's growth to another's self-condemnation.
D) One character's growth to another's sadness.

4) The primary function of the fourth and fifth paragraphs is to

A) Explain a reasoning and its outcome.
B) Express disciplinary actions and their origins.
C) Define a methodology and its response.
D) Describe a course of action and its consequences.

5) Over the course of the passage, the focus shifts from

A) A man's interaction with his daughter to his dreary work with her.
B) A man's enjoyment with his daughter to his regretful actions to her.
C) A man's experiences with his daughter to her irresponsibly playfulness.
 D) A description of an outing to the inside of a workshop.

Questions 1-5 are based on the following passage is adapted from Transcript of President Dwight D. Eisenhower's Farewell Address from https://www.ourdocuments.gov/

A vital element in keeping the peace is our military establishment. Our arms must be mighty, ready for instant action, so that no potential aggressor may be tempted to risk his own destruction.

5   Our military organization today bears little relation to that known by any of my predecessors in peacetime, or indeed by the fighting men of World War II or Korea.

Until the latest of our world conflicts, the United
10   States had no armaments industry. American makers of plowshares could, with time and as required, make swords as well. But now we can no longer risk emergency improvisation of national defense; we have been compelled to create a permanent
15   armaments industry of vast proportions. Added to this, three and a half million men and women are directly engaged in the defense establishment. We annually spend on military security more than the net income of all United State corporations.

20   This conjunction of an immense military establishment and a large arms industry is new in the American experience. The total influence - economic, political, even spiritual - is felt in every city, every state house, every office of the Federal government.
25   We recognize the imperative need for this development. Yet we must not fail to comprehend its grave implications. Our toil, resources, and livelihood are all involved; so is the very structure of our society.

30   In the councils of government, we must guard against the acquisition of unwarranted influence, whether sought or unsought, by the military-industrial complex. The potential for the disastrous rise of misplaced power exists and will persist.

35   We must never let the weight of this combination endanger our liberties or democratic processes. We should take nothing for granted only an alert and knowledgeable citizenry can compel the proper meshing of huge industrial and military machinery of
40   defense with our peaceful methods and goals, so that security and liberty may prosper together.

Akin to, and largely responsible for the sweeping changes in our industrial-military posture, has been the technological revolution during recent decades.
45   In this revolution, research has become central; it also becomes more formalized, complex, and costly. A steadily increasing share is conducted for, by, or at the direction of, the Federal government.

Today, the solitary inventor, tinkering in his shop,
50   has been overshadowed by task forces of scientists in laboratories and testing fields. In the same fashion, the free university, historically the fountainhead of free ideas and scientific discovery, has experienced a revolution in the conduct of research. Partly because
55   of the huge costs involved, a government contract becomes virtually a substitute for intellectual curiosity. For every old blackboard, there are now hundreds of new electronic computers.

The prospect of domination of the nation's
60   scholars by Federal employment, project allocations, and the power of money is ever present and is gravely to be regarded.

Yet, in holding scientific research and discovery in respect, as we should, we must also be alert to the
65   equal and opposite danger that public policy could itself become the captive of a scientific-technological elite.

It is the task of statesmanship to mold, to balance, and to integrate these and other forces, new and old,
70   within the principles of our democratic system-ever aiming toward the supreme goals of our free society.

1) The passage primarily serves to

A) Brief the nation on the military strides taken by the U.S.
B) Explain the need for military expansion.
C) Alert the Federal government of a possible military overthrow.
D) Warn the citizens of a military-government merger.

2) The main purpose of the opening sentence of the passage is to

A) Define the military's purpose.
B) Acknowledge the need for a military to maintain peace.
C) Provide context for the passage.
D) Juxtapose both peace and military for purposes of irony.

3) The central idea of the fifth paragraph is that

A) The U.S. must be careful not to be influenced by any forces.
B) Government should not be controlled by the military.
C) The military must guard the government against all influencing force.
D) Power can be a destructive force if not checked.

4) The primary function of the seventh and eighth paragraphs is to

A) Warn of the military using technology wrongly.
B) Note that the military has changed due to government sponsored technology.
C) State a need for the military to advance its use of technology.
D) Advise that military revolutions take place due to technological advances.

5) The main idea of the final paragraph is that

A) States must take control of leadership rather than the Federal government.
B) States need to use all powers necessary to prevent a governmental takeover.
C) Balance in government is important for the government to work well.
D) Government must manage its components to maintain a free society.

Questions 1-5 are based on the following passage adapted from *Taming a wandering attention: Short-form mindfulness training in student cohorts,* an article published in Frontiers in Human Neuroscience.

Mindfulness is a mental mode characterized by attention to present moment experience without conceptual elaboration or reactivity. Mindfulness training (MT) programs offer practices and didactic
5 discussions on how to stabilize and focus attention on one's present moment experience, as opposed to ruminating about the past or worrying about the future. A common practice offered in MT courses is mindfulness of breathing.

10 In this practice, the participant is instructed to focus on a selected sensation of breathing, e.g., the coolness of air in the nostrils, and maintain attention on that selected object for the period of formal practice. If a participant notices that his or her
15 attention has wandered to off-task thoughts, feelings, sensations, or other internal preoccupations, he or she is instructed to guide attention back to the target object, e.g., the breath. Therefore, this type of training includes explicit instructions to notice mind
20 wandering and respond by redirecting selective attention.

Given the centrality of addressing mind wandering in MT practices, prior studies have investigated if there are neural correlates to suggest that long-term
25 MT practice may reduce mind wandering. A study compared long-term meditation practitioners' and meditation naïve controls' neural activity in the default mode network, a network of brain regions implicated in mind wandering and self-related
30 processing. The results suggested that this network was relatively deactivated in the long-term practitioners relative to novices during a formal meditation practice period in the scanner. Long-term practitioners also subjectively reported less mind
35 wandering during meditation practice relative to controls. While this is consistent with the prediction that MT may reduce mind wandering, neural activity patterns and subjective experience sampling alone are insufficient to conclude that MT reduces mind
40 wandering. In addition, since this was a cross-sectional study, the possibility that long-term practitioners may intrinsically differ in their default mode functioning rather than having acquired

changes through their engagement in MT cannot be
45 ruled out.

A recent study investigated MT in a randomized control design with an active comparison group and asked whether MT administered to novices improves task performance and reduces reports of the
50 subjective experience of mind wandering. They offered a short-form MT course and a nutrition course to undergraduate college students. Performance on verbal Graduate Record Examination (GRE) subsections was higher and self-
55 reported mind wandering was lower in the MT group following training, a pattern not reported in the nutrition group. In addition to MT's benefits on the GRE, a real-world measure of academic mastery, task performance on the operation span task, a
60 laboratory measure of working memory capacity, was assessed. Consistent with other reports showing that MT bolsters working memory, only the MT group improved in their operation span scores.

Additionally, retrospective mind wandering
65 reports completed following the operation span task suggested that the MT group and not the nutrition group showed lower mind wandering during the working memory task after the intervention than before it. A mediation analysis demonstrated that
70 self-reported mind wandering significantly mediated the effect of MT on operation span and GRE performance, driven by those who had higher mind wandering prior to training. Accordingly, the authors concluded that the increase in performance may be
75 attributable to a reduction in mind wandering. This proposal is consistent with a growing literature suggesting that working memory and mind wandering are interrelated.

While prior studies of MT in academic settings
80 suggest it is beneficial, no studies have examined the impact of MT on optimizing task performance and reducing mind wandering over the course of the academic semester in University students. There is growing evidence that students' stress levels and
85 dysphoria increase over the semester, especially as they approach exams. Off-task thinking has been related to psychological distress, as well as negative vs. neutral mood and as such, it is possible that mind wandering may increase over the semester as well.
90 Here, we ask if MT may help to curb mind wandering that may result from rising academic pressures over the semester.

1) The first paragraph serves mostly to

A) Explain a technical term.
B) Elaborate on a point in subsequent paragraphs.
C) Offer an explanation of the topic.
D) Compel the reader to side with the author's point of view.

2) The main idea of the second paragraph is

A) Why Mindfulness training works.
B) The effects of Mindfulness training.
C) How Mindfulness training develops the brain.
D) The methodology of Mindfulness training.

3) The central idea of the third paragraph is

A) Addressing the centrality of Mindfulness training.
B) A study on Mindfulness training.
C) The effects of long-term practice of Mindfulness training.
D) Complications of Mindfulness training.

4) The primary function of the fourth and fifth paragraphs is to

A) Summarize the findings of a study.
B) Note how Mindfulness training is administered to novices.
C) Describe the effects of Mindfulness training on tasks and mind wandering.
D) Explain the reasoning of how Mindfulness training affects the brain.

5) Which choice best summarizes the passage?

A) Mindfulness training is a new mental practice that distracts people from their daily lives and allows illusions to develop.
B) Mindfulness training is a method that allows people to subtract thoughts from their minds.
C) Mindfulness training is a mental practice that has been shown to have deleterious effects.
D) Mindfulness training is a mental practice that helps people with task performance and the mind's wandering.

Questions 1-5 are based on the following passage adapted from *The La Chance Mine* Mystery by Susan Carleton Jones.

Little as I guessed it, this story really began at Skunk's Misery. But Skunk's Misery was the last thing in my head, though I had just come from the place.

Hungry, dog-tired, cross with the crossness of a
5   man in authority whose orders have been forgotten or disregarded, I drove Billy Jones's old canoe across Lac Tremblant on my way home to Dudley Wilbraham's gold mine at La Chance, after an absence of months. It was halfway to dark, and the
10 bitter November wind blew dead in my teeth. Slaps of spray from flying wave-crests blinded me with gouts of lake water, that was oddly warm till the cutting wind froze it to a coating of solid ice on my bare hands and stinging face, that I had to keep
15 dabbing on my paddling shoulder to get my eyes clear in order that I might stare in front of my leaky, borrowed canoe.

To a stranger there might have seemed to be nothing particular to stare at, out on a lake where
20 the world was all wind and lumpy seas and growing November twilight; but anyone who had lived at La Chance knew better. By the map, Lac Tremblant should have been our nearest gold route to civilization, but it was a lake that was no lake, as far
25 as transport was concerned, and we never used it. The five-mile crossing I was making was just a fair sample of the forty miles of length Lac Tremblant stretched mockingly past the La Chance mine toward the main road from Caraquet—our nearest
30 settlement—to railhead: and that was forty miles of rough water, sown with rocks that were sometimes visible as tombstones in a cemetery and sometimes hidden like rattlesnakes in a blanket. For the depth of Lac Tremblant, or its fairway, were two things no
35 man might ever count on. It would fall in a night to shallows a child could wade through, among bristling needles of rocks no one had ever guessed at; and rise in a morning to the tops of the spruce scrub on its banks,—a sweet spread of water with not a rock
40 to be seen. What hidden spring fed it was a mystery. But in the bitterest winter it was never cold enough to freeze, further than to form surging masses of frazil ice that would neither let a canoe push through them nor yet support the weight of a man. Winter or
45 summer, it was no thoroughfare—and neither was

the ungodly jumble of swamp and mountains that stopped me from tapping the lower end of it—or I should not have spent the last three months in making fifty miles of road through untrodden bush to
50 Caraquet, over which to transport the La Chance gold to a post-road and a railway: and it was no chosen return route of mine to La Chance now, either.

If I could draw you a map I should not have to
55 explain the country. But failing that I will be as clear as I can. The line of Lac Tremblant, and that of the road I had just made from Caraquet to La Chance, ran away from each other in two sides of a triangle,—except that the La Chance mine was five
60 miles down the far side of the lake from Caraquet, and my road had to half-moon around the head of Lac Tremblant to get home—a lavish curve, too, by reason of swamps.

But it was on that half-moon road that I should
65 have been now, if my order to have a horse meet me at the Halfway Stables, I had built at the beginning of it had not been forgotten or disregarded by someone at La Chance.

Getting drenched to the skin with lake water was
70 no rattling good exchange for riding home on a fresh horse that felt like a warm stove under me, but a five-mile short cut across the apex of the road and lake triangle was better than walking twenty-two miles along the side of it on my own legs.

75 I was obliged to get home, for reasons of my own; but when I walked in on Billy Jones, the foreman at the Halfway stables, that afternoon, after months of absence, there was not even one team horse in his stables. There was not a soul about the place, either,
80 but Billy himself, blandly idle and sprawling over a grubby old newspaper in front of the stove in his shack.

I was as sick of the bush as I was of the shack. I wanted a place of my own and a life of my own: and I
85 was going to have it. There was nothing but old friendship to tie me to Wilbraham's; I could do as well anywhere else, and I was going there tomorrow; going somewhere, anyhow, so that when my day's work was over I could go home to a blazing fire on a
90 wide hearth, my own roof over my head, and land I could call my own.

1) The passage primarily serves to

A) Entertain the reader with a man's hardships.
B) Narrate a man's journey through rough country.
C) Account of a man's journey back home.
D) Build up the conflict of the story.

2) The primary function of the fifth and sixth paragraphs (lines 64-74) is to

A) Recollect the time the main character spent in the bush.
B) Describe the hardship of the main character.
C) Illustrate the treacherous journey and the dilemmas the main character undergoes.
D) Present the setting the main character faces.

3) The primary purpose of lines 22-25 ("By ... it") is to

A) Express the people's opinion of the lake being incorrectly thought of as a lake.
B) Point out that the lake was unlike an average lake due to water irregularities.
C) Negate its lake-like properties and relate it to an underused resource.
D) Explain how people felt about misnomers in relation to transport.

4) What function does the seventh paragraph in the passage as a whole?

A) It prolongs the main character's journey to his destination.
B) It continues the main character's hardships in the story.
C) It illustrates a change in the main character's perception of his circumstances.
D) It gives an overview of a problem.

5) Over the course of the passage, the focus shifts from
A) Hardships to comfort.
B) Struggle to fulfillment.
C) Venture to arrival.
D) Suffering to abeyance.

Questions 1-5 are based on the following passage adapted from *The Spirit of Youth and the City Streets* by Jane Addams.

There are many city neighborhoods in which practically every young person who has attained the age of fourteen years enters a factory. When the work itself offers nothing of interest, and when no public provision is made for recreation, the situation becomes almost insupportable to the youth whose ancestors have been rough-working and hard-playing peasants.

In such neighborhoods, the joy of youth is well-nigh extinguished; and in that long procession of factory workers, each morning and evening, the young walk almost as wearily and listlessly as the old. Young people working in modern factories situated in cities dominated by the ideals of Capitalism face a combination which tends almost irresistibly to overwhelm the spirit of youth.

When people lived on farms and villages where, although youthful pleasures might be frowned upon and crushed out, the young people still had a chance to find self-expression in their work. Plowing the field and spinning the flax could be carried on with a certain joyousness and vigor which the organization of modern industry too often precludes. Present industry, based upon the inventions of the nineteenth century, has little connection with the old patterns in which men have worked for generations. The modern factory calls for an expenditure of nervous energy almost more than it demands muscular effort, or at least machinery so far performs the work of the massive muscles, that greater stress is laid upon fine and exact movements necessarily involving nervous strain. But these movements are exactly of the type to which the muscles of a growing boy least readily respond, quite as the admonition to be accurate and faithful is that which appeals the least to his big primitive emotions. The demands made upon his eyes are complicated and trivial, the use of his muscles is fussy and monotonous, the relation between cause and effect is remote and obscure. Apparently no one is concerned as to what may be done to aid him in this process and to relieve it of its dullness and difficulty, to mitigate its strain and harshness.

Perhaps never before have young people been expected to work from motives so detached from direct emotional incentive. Never has the age of marriage been so long delayed; never has the work of youth been so separated from the family life and the public opinion of the community. Education alone can repair these losses. It alone has the power of organizing a child's activities with some reference to the life he will later lead and of giving him a clue as to what to select and what to eliminate when he comes into contact with contemporary social and industrial conditions. And until educators take hold of the situation, the rest of the community is powerless.

In vast regions of the city which are completely dominated by the factory, it is as if the development of industry had outrun all the educational and social arrangements.

The revolt of youth against uniformity and the necessity of following careful directions laid down by someone else, many times results in such nervous irritability that the youth, in spite of all sorts of prudential reasons, "throws up his job," if only to get outside the factory walls into the freer street, just as the narrowness of the school enclosure induces many a boy to jump the fence.

When the boy is on the street, however, and is "standing around on the corner" with the gang to which he mysteriously attaches himself, he finds the difficulties of direct untrammeled action almost as great there as they were in the factory, but for an entirely different set of reasons. The necessity so strongly felt in the factory for an outlet to his sudden and furious bursts of energy, his overmastering desire to prove that he could do things "without being bossed all the time," finds little chance for expression, for he discovers that in whatever really active pursuit he tries to engage, he is promptly suppressed by the police. After several futile attempts at self-expression, he returns to his street corner subdued and so far discouraged that when he has the next impulse to vigorous action he concludes that it is of no use, and sullenly settles back into inactivity. He thus learns to persuade himself that it is better to do nothing, or, as the psychologist would say, "to inhibit his motor impulses."

1) The central idea of the passage is that

A) Youth do not have emotional outlets due to labor.
B) Youth are overworked in the cities.
C) The need for workers has corrupted the youth.
D) Capitalism is forcing the youth to work at earlier ages sacrificing their innocence.

2) The main purpose of lines 9-10 ("In ... extinguished;") is to

A) Establish that youth work to extinguish unnecessary aspects of their lives.
B) Describe the uselessness of the lives of youth.
C) Negate the premise made in the first paragraph.
D) Depict the unfortunate circumstances of youth.

3) During the course of the first paragraph, the narrator's focus shifts from

A) The past to the present.
B) The ways the older generations relieved stress to the current youths' inability to.
C) How past peoples portrayed themselves through work to the current work's stifling of youth.
D) Methods of work in the past to current innovations.

4) The central idea of the fourth paragraph is that

A) Youth have changed from the past to the present.
B) Never have the youth had such difficulties.
C) Education is the solution to solving the youth's problems.
D) Educators do not care enough to change the circumstances of youth.

5) The primary function of the sixth and seventh paragraphs is to

A) Explain what happens to youth if they can no longer tolerate factory life.
B) Describe ways that youth are able to escape the trend of their peers.
C) Inspire rebellious thoughts in those who wish to be free of Capitalistic servitude.
D) Propose alternatives to the stresses youth sustain in factory life.

Answer Keys

Single Paragraph starter exercises with 2 questions and web-chart

Sewage Treatment (Pg.2)

1) B - The text says, "land which is being treated for the ...time." means the longer the land has been used for sewage treatment, the land purifies it better. (Using the Contrapositive of the original statement) The text continues "...absorbing powers, which gradually ripen until they have reached maximum efficiency." means by using the soil more it "ripens" or alters for better sewage take in and processing.

2) B - The first sentence is about the land that is more often used for sewage treatment is more efficient, this is a process. The second sentence is about how the soil filters the sewage and absorbs oxygen, which is a process in sewage treatment. The third sentence is about the depth the sewage that goes into the soil and the factors, part of the process of sewage treatment. The final sentence is about the need for "careful management" of these processes to avoid out-flow into underdrains. So, the whole passage in one way or another is about the process that sewage is filtered.

A Short History of the World by H. G. Wells (Pg.3)

1) C - The point of the paragraph is to say that choosing Versailles as the location to hold the peace conference for ending WW1 was bad because that was the location that Germany proclaimed, told all, about their coming together as a united Germany, an empire. So, holding the end of the German empire in the same place as it started in an embarrassment; therefore, C, the purpose of the passage is to recognize a failed initiative. (Initiative means a plan to solve a problem, that problem being concluding WW1.)

2) A - Melodramatic means to do or say in a way that is extreme or exaggerated. So, the reversal of the 1871 proclamation of the German Empire by condemning Germany in the same place is extreme and exaggerated. The use of the Hall of Mirrors, a special room, where the treaty was signed, is added to show how the reversal was so humiliating.

The Story of Doctor Dolittle (Pg.4)

1) B - Disorienting means confused, lost, that's the description given in the story. Then the story switches to them being caught by the king's men, which is worse than being lost.

2) C - Being caught by the king's men is worse than being lost because the people being caught are at the mercy of the king.

The Fireside Chats (Pg.5)

1) A - A politician is a person who campaigns for or holds a position in government such as a Congressman or a President. In the text, the president is informing how the banking institution uses money to invest, but has a small amount for withdrawal by customers.

2) A - The text says there's a small amount of money in the bank for the customers. So, the main idea of that sentence is to illustrate the quantity of funds available in banks.

Voyager 1 Encounters Saturn by NASA (Pg.6)

1) A - Pique means to interest, and the words and phrases such as "No other generation" and "to reach beyond our world" and "hear the forces that shape our universe" used in the first sentence are to interest the reader. Also, the repetition of the word "to" gives a sense of awe which is to interest the reader.

2) D - The first sentence tells what NASA has done by going into space. The next sentence states again that NASA explored 5 planets. The next sentence is about exploring planets and their properties and finally a new launch.

The Wonderful Wizard of Oz (Pg.7)

1) D - Most of the paragraph describes something about the area where the cyclone set the house down such as " lovely patches of greensward", "Banks of gorgeous flowers", "brilliant plumage of... trees", a small brook"; all describing the setting.

2) C - A cyclone is a destructive natural event that destroys houses and buildings, so for it to "set the house down very gently" is irregular for a natural event.

Ronald Reagan (Pg.8)

1) B - Most of the paragraph is about how money is spent by the government. Then Reagan clearly states, "Simple fairness dictates that government must not raise taxes on families struggling to pay their bills."

2) C - Reagan is saying that the problem is that the government's share is greater than what the people can afford. Answer choice C express this best.

Household Diary Summary, Mail Markets (Pg.9)

1) D - The primary purpose is to summarize, or give an overview, about the USPS mail based on the markets it serves, or delivers mail, as stated in the first sentence

2) D - The first three sentences is the breakdown of the "decline" or "reduction" stated in answer choice D. The rest of the paragraph explains about the reasons for its decline as stated in line 16, "decline in correspondence."

Challenges for Uneven-Aged Silviculture in Restoration (Pg.10)

1) D - Resistance, for something to fight against something to live, and resilience, staying strong, are all about being healthy, then the text states how forest management and silvicultural systems are used to keep forest strands strong, or in other words healthy.

2) C - The article states that, "The resistance and resilience of forest stands to disturbance are strongly influenced by forest management and the type of silvicultural system used" which means that these 2 systems are being used to keep forests strong, or "maintaining strong forests" stated in C. Then the middle section is about examples of these systems followed by where it is happening in Europe.

Adventures in American Bookshops (Pg.11)

1) C- Although the first sentence states a rich person, what he is doing is actually buying throughout the 1st paragraph as in: "once becomes a victim to the craze for an artistic home" meaning he buys an artistic home. Also, "his artistic desires speak of art and rugs and paintings" means he buys arts and paintings, continuing on with "Mr. So-and-So who spent thousands of dollars for antique furniture or for pictures in auctions, and he begins his walks on these dangerous and costly grounds." This newly rich person hears that some other person (Mr. So-and-So) buys thousands of dollars worth of items, and so does he. Lastly, he says that with all of the money he spends, he buys the reputation of the art dealer as well as the wrapping paper and string (which obviously does not come free). He is the buyer and not just a rich person. The next paragraph is about the antique dealer getting to go to houses to buy "rubbish", antiques that only he would know are antiques from his expertise, such as paintings by Rubens or Tintoretto or Martha Washington's wedding slippers or a suite of magnificent Colonial furniture. The text ends with "sure enough these are red-letter days for almost every antique dealer." meaning that antique dealers get a special day. So, the entire 2nd paragraph is about the seller to the buyer, who is the antique dealer.

2) A - Simply, the text is saying that he gets access to an estate. Then he looks at the "rubbish" to find unknown high valued items, which are really good according to the idiom "red-letter-days", meaning any day of special significance or opportunity.

Fill in the Blank Questions:

Self-Reliance (Pg.12)

1. Emphasize that people should follow their own will to do what they want, trust themselves, and be natural with who they are; In short, to be self-reliant on themselves.

2. To trust in one's self in how they live life.

3. To show that even babies, children, and animals are the perfect examples of the best way to approach the world because they are aware of their emotions and show them without thought of how they are perceived. By doing this, they are mentally, or emotionally, self-reliant on themselves, unlike adults.

4. How boys are independent and self-reliant to how man (adults) is self-conscious and inhibits himself from expressing his true feelings; thus being controlled by the norms of society.

5. In the previous paragraph, Emerson tells about how boys are free (Ln 78-83" Ah,...affairs), these are the voices he is referring to, but as we grow up and enter society, these voices become less a driving force in our lives.

6. Summarize the ideas in the passage by saying that society changes people to fit into society and self-reliance is not wanted.

Home Life of Great Authors with a focus on Washington Irving (Pg.14)

1. Discuss Washington Irving and the development of his career.

2. Express the concerns of Washington's father about his actions coming from the devil.

3. Washington talking about his bad health to his experiences in Europe with Allston.

4. His shift in focus from art scheme to his literary work.

5. An example of how Washington's literary work had made him famous.

6. His successful life after returning to New York.

The Extermination of The American Bison *(Pg.16)*

1. State that American bison were the most abundant animals, but at the time of the writing of the text, nearly became extinct.

2. Introduce the idea that there were a lot of American Bison.

3. It gives eye witness accounts of the innumerable number of American Bison in many parts of the U.S.

4. The purpose is to transition from the massive amounts stated in the previous paragraph with the eventual extermination of the American bison.

5. Give specific reasons for the decrease of the American bison population.

6. Describing the massive amounts of American Bison in the U.S. to the extermination of them and its cause.

The Chemistry of Food and Nutrition *(Pg.18)*

1. Food can lose nutritional value and taste if over prepared.

2. Define food as a nutriment that enters only through the intestinal canal by adding a restriction to all other ways that nutriments can enter the body.

3. Informing of what minerals come from food to specifics about their nutritional value.

4. Describe an experiment that when foods are boiled or soaked in water lose minerals and taste.

5. Absorbs minerals from food thus leaving food less nutritious.

6. By boiling food, the food is less tasty; therefore, table salt must be added for taste which causes health problems. He explains other ways of cooking to decrease loss of natural minerals.

Great Men and Famous Women: William the 1st *(Pg.20)*

1. Describe William's difficulties as a young Duke and the battles he fought.

2. Establish that William's father named William his heir, thus the source of his difficulties described later in the passage.

3. The second paragraph provides information of his early difficulties, an alliance to save him, and how that alliance would later threaten his position.

4. Explain his connections for power by marrying the Earl of Flanders' daughter and the legal opposition to it.

5. Describe William's difficulty in the face of the overwhelming odds of the king's and other great adversaries' armies.

6. Summarize William's battles to protect his lands against the King and other adversaries and introduce his greatest victory.

Proverbs and Their Lessons (Pg.22)

1) B - The first paragraph states that many people use them in line 6 "We think of them but as sayings on the lips of the multitude" and that we use them a lot and for a long time in line 7 and 8 "not a few of them have been familiar to us as far back as we can remember". In the second paragraph, in lines 30-32 the text states, "The fact that they please the people, and have pleased them for ages" meaning that people have liked proverbs for a long time. It continues with "[Proverbs have been] borne safely upon the waters of that great stream of time, which has swallowed so much beneath its waves" meaning that over time many things have been lost to humans, but proverbs have lasted because of their importance to people. In the third paragraph, the author states that some of the most influential thinkers and writers have used and written about and with proverbs.

2) B - Throughout lines 6-20 the text states numerous times that we know them, but not the real meaning of them. "We think of them but as sayings on the lips of the multitude" meaning many people use them. Also, "not a few of them have been familiar to us as far back as we can remember." Not a few means many are known to us for a long time. The author continues by saying that "we yet have remained blind in the main to the wit, wisdom, and imagination, of which they are full; and very little conscious of the amusement, instruction, insight, which they are capable of yielding." This means that we don't understand the "wit, wisdom, and imagination" or "the amusement, instruction, insight."
Lastly the author writes, "Unless too we have devoted a certain attention to the subject, we shall not be at all aware how little those more familiar ones, which are frequent on the lips of men, exhaust the treasure of our native proverbs." Unless effort is put into knowing what they mean, we will just continue to use them, thus supporting the idea that people do not understand the depth of proverbs.

3) D - In lines 27-28 the text states " And yet there is much to induce us to reconsider our judgment... should we be thus tempted to slight them...unworthy of a serious attention " Meaning that we should rethink our wrong thinking about them as simple things and should pay attention to them. The first part of the sentence states we should reconsider then the rest of the sentence states the negative points which are countered by the first part of the sentence.

4) B - In lines 45-48 the author writes of different educated people or intellectuals as "the greatest poets, the most profound philosophers, the most learned scholars, the most genial writers." Then on line 51, the author shifts to the upper classes' disdain for proverbs as stated by Lord Chesterfield in "no man of fashion... ever uses a proverb."

5) C - The second part of the third paragraph says that the upper class did not use proverbs. The entire fourth paragraph is examples of the people who did: Aristotle, Shakespeare, Cervantes, Plautus, Rabelais, Montaigne, and Coleridge.

The History of Women's Suffrage Vol 1. (Pg.24)

1) A - In the first paragraph, lines 4-8 states, "political and religious revolutions in France, Germany, Italy, and America; and their tendency to substitute for the divine right of kings, priests, and orders of nobility, the higher and broader one of individual conscience and judgment". Which means that of kings, priests, and orders of nobility lost their power to people's individual conscience and judgment (The revolutions and national changes) In the second paragraph, lines 34 to 36, the test states " the Protestant Reformation roused woman, as well as man, to new and higher thought....The bold declarations of Luther..." led to "individual judgment above church authority", then the text moves to science by saying that humans are the most important of nature's last work, thus saying that the individual man and woman are the focus, again individualism, " The revelations of science, too, analysing and portraying the wonders and beauties of this material world, crowned with new dignity, man and woman,—Nature's last and proudest work. Combe and Spurzheim, proving by their phrenological discoveries that the feelings, sentiments, and affections of the soul, mold and shape the skull, gave new importance to woman's thought as mother of the race. Each of these movements, the revolutionary wars and national changes, the religious movement, the scientific movement led to individualism which eventually leads to women receiving the right to vote in the suffrage movement.

2) C - In lines 3-6 the text states that "the liberal social ideas" which bring about "the higher and broader one of individual conscience and judgment in all matters" or in other words individualism, replace the kings, priests, and nobility which are the authoritarian structures as stated in "substitute for the divine right of kings, priests, and orders of nobility".

3) C - In line 59 it states the subject "The revelations of science" then the text continues to how the child's mother's "feelings, sentiments, and affections of the soul, mold and shape the skull of a child", then ending the sentence with "gave new importance to woman's thought as mother of the race." So women, "the mother of the (human) race", mold the skull of a child (during pregnancy) through her "feelings, sentiments, and affections of the soul" meaning that the mother forms the baby with her emotions.

4) C - In lines 82-83 the text states "the immediate causes that led to the demand for the equal political rights of women" which means that the author is trying to "explain" the reasons for the insistence of the suffrage movement "equal political rights of women".

5) A - The text states in line 8 that many factors led to the realization of "individual conscience and judgment". Then in paragraph 2 lines 37, the text says that again other factors led to, "individual judgment above church authority". Again, in paragraph 3 lines 67, even more factors led to "tending to individualism, " All of this led the shift in lines 60-65 "And when in the progress of civilization, the time had fully come for the recognition of the feminine element in humanity, women, in every civilized country unknown to each other, began simultaneously to demand a broader sphere of action." Meaning that civilization progressed to recognize women, then the passage continues with the next idea of the text that although it has not been achieved, lines 75 to 81 "Hence the woman's suffrage movement has not yet been accepted as the legitimate outgrowth of American ideas—a component part of the history of our republic—but is falsely considered the willful outburst of a few unbalanced minds, whose ideas can never be realized under any form of government". The time for suffrage has come and is gaining support as stated throughout the final paragraph.

Distribution of Animals (Pg.26)

1) C - The first paragraph talks about how birds and mammals of certain areas are alike, paragraphs 2, 3, 4, and 5 all discuss how birds evolved differently due to migrating to islands:

Paragraph 2: "Yet these barriers have not been absolute; and in the course of ages birds have been able to reach almost every habitable land upon the globe," and "abound in birds, often of peculiar types and remarkable for some unusual character or habit."

Paragraph 3: "Thus, we have the Pigeons and the Parrots most wonderfully developed in the Australian region, which is pre-eminently insular; and both these groups here acquire conspicuous colors very unusually, or altogether absent, elsewhere. Similar colors (black and red) appear, in the same two groups, in the distant Mascarene Islands; while in the Antilles the parrots have often white heads, a character not found in the allied species on the South American continent."

Paragraph 4: "Again, birds exhibit to us a remarkable contrast as regards the oceanic islands of tropical and temperate latitudes; for a while most of the former present hardly any cases of specific identity with the birds of adjacent continents, the latter often show hardly any differences."

Paragraph 5: "They also throw much light on the relationship between distribution and the external characters of animals;"

2) A - The 1st sentence states, "Although birds are, of all land-vertebrates, the best able to cross seas and oceans, it is remarkable how closely the main features of their distribution correspond with those of the Mammals", which means birds can fly and are most suitable for long distance, over-water travel, and that the way that birds and mammals are distributed in areas is related to the fact that birds can travel those distances.

3) B - In the last line it states, "more light thrown upon their past history by means of their birds". "More light thrown upon" means to reveal, or tell about, about the history of the islands by birds. So, the author is declaring that the birds have revealed more about the island than the birds. This is because the birds made an impact on telling the history of the island.

4) C - In lines 43- 46, the text states, "Another peculiar feature in the distribution of this class is the extraordinary manner in which certain groups and certain external characteristics, have become developed in islands, " which is explaining that certain groups and external characteristics have developed on islands. It continues with a further explanation that, "where the smaller and less powerful birds have been protected from the incursions of mammals' enemies, and where rapacious birds—which seem to some degree dependent on the abundance of mammals—are also scarce," meaning that the birds on those islands have been protected from not being prey to mammals and large birds that eat those mammals. Then the shift begins with examples of the developments in lines 50-64.

5) B - In lines 79-82, the article states, "they give us much curious and suggestive information as to the various and complex modes in which the existing peculiarities of the distribution of animals have been brought about," meaning that birds tell us about how their distribution, or dispersion, makes special differences, or peculiarities. It continues with, "They also throw much light on the relation between distribution and the external characters of animals," meaning how they look different than other similar birds.

Economy by Henry David Thoreau (Pg.28)

1) A - Paragraph 1 talks about how we should not be a slave, or a slave to ourselves. The opening sentence of paragraph 2 states that the man is divine in the form of a string of questions. He has much to do, but he must do his responsibilities. Paragraph 3 is about man's thoughts about himself is what makes his fate; he himself makes his own fate. Paragraph 4 is about man's desperation in life. Paragraph 5 is about most men live a common life because there is no other choice. Paragraph 6 is about how much the old have NOTHING to teach the young. Lastly, the seventh paragraph is a story showing the ignorance of man. So, paragraphs 1-3 are about man needing not be a slave to himself, being divine and has many responsibilities and that man makes his own fate, his life, all of these need confidence to realize and do. Paragraphs 4 and 5 are about man living in desperation in a common life, therefore Thoreau is suggesting that people must take control of their lives, live deliberately. Thoreau continues that same line of thought in paragraph 6 that the youth should do things and not learn from the old people, again suggesting living a life that they choose and live; thus living deliberately.

2) C - The main idea of this sentence is that people are more critical of themselves than any others. If we switch the sentence around, we get: our own private, or personal, opinion is a strong tyrant compared to public opinion. By rearranging the sentence, we can see that C s the correct answer.

3) B - The second paragraph makes it obvious that B is correct because the questions are about man's "duty", "destiny" concluding with man's opinion of himself is strong. The third paragraph starts with "with what a man thinks of himself determines ... his fate." Then it talks about slaves' and ladies' fates, all having to do with man's existence and how he lives it.

4) A - As in the answer explanation for question 1, this whole paragraph is about how much the old have NOTHING to teach the young, so A is the closest. There are too many examples to cite here. Read the paragraph again and underline the points Thoreau makes about having nothing to learn from old people.

5) D - A dichotomy is defined as something that seems to have contradictory qualities. The fact that the farmer believes that he must supply "...his system with the raw material of bones" while " walking all the while he talks behind his oxen, which, with vegetable-made bones..." is contradictory, or statements that oppose each other. The oxen eats only vegetables and has strong bones, but the farmer thinks he needs bone-making material is a dichotomy, or contradictory.

Reconstruction (Pg.30)

1) D - Douglas says that sometimes rebellion can be needed in line 1, "There is cause to be thankful even for rebellion." He continues saying that it never comes before it is needed, meaning it is the last resort in lines 4-5, " It is an instructor never a day before its time..." and continues on with" for it comes only when all other means of progress and enlightenment have failed." Continuing his point that it is a last resort because all other means "have failed"

2) C - Ruination means the state of being ruined. The passage states that the Southern states were "exhausted, beaten, conquered," which for states means being ruined and the sentence continues with " they fell powerless at the feet of Federal authority" continuing the point that they had no power and were "at the feet" of the Federal government meaning they were begging. All of this points to the answer being ruination.

3) B - A disclaimer is a statement that says what something is not, or does not have the purpose to do, so lines 23-25 state, "It is not, however, within the scope of this paper to point out the precise steps to be taken, and the means to be employed." It's disclaiming that this paper is not to say what to do. The next lines 25-27 continue that thought with "The people are less concerned about these than the grand end to be attained," meaning the people are not concerned with the "steps", but with the end that will be gained. The rest of the paragraph is about doing something to reach that end, a call to action. This can be seen in the phrase "They demand..." (line 27), "They want" (line 32) and that call to action is "The South must be opened to the light of law

and liberty" (lines 39-40). So, a disclaimer telling what the essay isn't to a call to action.

4) C - The author is clear that what is needed to make the South functional again for black and white people is to transform, make a thorough change, of the structure of the South's governing structure as in line 43, "The plain, common-sense way of doing this work"; he is not wishy-washy or unsure.

5) A - Lines 73-74 discuss the Constitution not distinguishing between state and U.S. (Federal) citizenship stating, "Neither does it know any difference between a citizen of a State and a citizen of the United States. Citizenship evidently includes all the rights of citizens, whether State or national." Then Douglas discusses how the previous Congress made a mistake in distinguishing between state and Federal citizenship, which allowed the Southern states to include, or exclude slaves as citizens for the states. The 3/5's compromise was when Southern states included their population of slaves to be counted as three-fifths of a white person in order to increase the population of their states so that those states would have many more seats in the House of Representatives and more representation in the Electoral College. Finally, it ends with, "so that a legal voter in any State shall be a legal voter in all the States". So, Douglas is saying that the Constitution should not tell the difference and distinguish between state and Federal citizenship.

Flexitarianism (Pg.32)

1) B- From the first sentence which calls flexitarianism a neoteric, meaning a new term, to it being added to "Oxford English Dictionary in 2014" also breaking flexitarian into its base words, and ending with an exact meaning, the entire paragraph is about defining the word.

2) A- "most closely in line with that of" mean is similar to, so the text is making a synonymous relationship between flexitarianism and semi/demi-vegetarianism.

3) C- The beginning of the paragraph starts with "The FD seems to recognize the fact that meat is an important source of protein, fat, and micronutrients" meaning that there are some benefits to eating meat, but then the sentence switches with the word "yet" in line 25 then talks about meat based diets being bad for animals' welfare and the remainder of the paragraph is about the diseases caused by meats. So C, both benefits and detriments (negative aspects), is correct.

4) A - The numbers in both paragraphs are data, statistics, and facts, but the constant usage of the word "reduce", "reducers", "reductions", "reduced" pair up with "reduction" in the answer choice. Then paragraph 6 talks about the higher and lower weight, the effects of being a non-vegetarians, strict vegetarians, lacto-ovo vegetarians, etc.

5) A - The first two paragraphs define what flexitarianism is - an eating lifestyle, the third paragraph is about meat causing diseases, the fourth paragraph is about people who are reducing their meat intake, the fifth paragraph is about plant-based diets in relation to weight loss, the sixth paragraph is about data on different eaters (vegetarians having the most weight loss) and the seventh paragraph is about the prevention and benefits. So, A is the best answer choice.

The Red Badge of Courage (Pg.34)

1) C - Paragraph 1 is about an army arising in the morning and the setting in the country-side. Paragraph 2 is about a soldier hearing a rumor of the army going into battle. Paragraph 3 is about groups of soldiers discussing the rumor. Paragraph 4 is about one man doubting the news and the rumor spreader defending his words. Paragraph 5 is about an officer doubting moving out, paragraph 6 is about soldiers' debate on hear say of generals and opposing rumors. Paragraph 7 is a dialog of a soldier who says the army will move out and another who doesn't. Paragraph 8 is about the rumor spreader getting soldiers excited by telling his proofs of the army moving out. Paragraph 9 is about the soldier goes to his quarters after hearing the rumor. Paragraph 10 is about the solder thinking about going to the war; the idea astonishes him. So, the entire passage is about soldiers' reactions of a rumor of moving out to battle.

2) B - The first paragraph talks about the landscape, changing from brown to green. A river of amber-tInted color, a stream, and camp-fires of opposing army in the hills. This is establishing (1st paragraph) the setting of the story.

3) D - It has been established that the news of moving out is a rumour. The first exclamation, "It's a lie!" establishes that the person does not believe in the rumour line 36 continues with " I don't believe... " So, disbelief in the rumour being spread is the answer.

4) D - The Corporal swearing means that he disapproves. For an officer to swear, he/she would have to be feeling negative feelings about that subject.

5) C - Both paragraphs started off with the same person, one youthful soldier. Line 70" There was a youthful private" and line 78 " The youth..." The last line states," He wished to be alone with some new thoughts..." and in lines 78-84 the text is about him being astonished that he would go to battle, he couldn't believe it (going to the battle) and being part of "great affairs of the earth" being war. So, the two paragraphs are about a soldier thinking, or ruminating, about fighting in a battle.

The Poor Man's Garden from Social Notes (Pg.36)

1) C - From line 4-14, most of the paragraph, the text tells of the different social gardening dividing it into the rich (line 4), the well-to-do, middle class,(line 5), and the dwellers in the one back room mearing the poor.

2) B - In lines 15-18, the text states "Flowers...mom the toilers of this city of brick and mortar are familiar with them the better for their mental and moral health." which is saying that the more the workers, toilers of the city are made familiar with flowers the better their mental and moral health will be the which are the benefits of the flowers. Lines 19-20 tell us that the rich have set the example, which is the origins that are in their house. So, B, the second paragraph is telling us the benefits of city gardening and the origins, being the rich.

3) A - Lines 32-37 tell how upper-class people have been "fastening this growing feeling" meaning helping to grow the feeling of window gardening, by "giving prizes for the best plants grown in dingy backyards and smokes garret-rooms" meaning they are giving prizes to people who are growing and doing city gardening. So, A, social events, like competitions or exhibitions have been set up to promote, encourage, city gardening.

4) B - In the seventh paragraph the text states that flower sermons, talks in a church, are given by Clergymen, men of religion, who have an interest in youth. The first paragraph continues with how Christ hallowed, blessed, flowers by name, all having to do with religion. Then in the eighth paragraph starts off with how "the culture of plants" benefits people, but then returns to the religious idea in the middle of the paragraph to the end in lines 64-70. So, B, the religious value of flowers is correct.

5) C - A call to action is telling people to do something. The author tells gardeners (line 81: To those...) and home gardeners (line 82-83: To the more homely...). Then the text says in line 85 " I say..."the "I say" is the call to acton in an old fashion way, then the author tells what he wants people to do, which is to garden in the city.

What Is Marine Biodiversity? (Pg.38)

1) B - The first three paragraphs are defining biodiversity including an overview of the environments that make up biodiversity, the fifth paragraph states the negative, then positive human activities, finally ending with the final paragraph talking about human attempts, through government assessments, to "achieve Good Environmental Status (GES)". So, B is the best answer choice.

2) D - The beginning phrase "the variability among living organisms from all sources" is an explanation of what biodiversity is meaning a lot of living things from all different areas. Then the sentence continues with examples of biodiversity such as land, ocean, and other water life-forms and their living environments: "terrestrial, marine, and other aquatic ecosystems and the ecological complexes of which they are part". So D is a definition and the three examples.

3) A - The first sentence of paragraph 3 opens with, "The structural aspect... ", then line 29 starts with "The structural aspect" so, the paragraph is discussing two aspects, the structural and the functional aspects of marine environments.

4) B - Again, the first four paragraphs deal with what biodiversity is and the last two paragraphs are about human activities and government intervention to assess environments.

5) A - The phrase "have been recently collated" means that they have already collected and combined, and "a method to select the most adequate has been proposed," means that they have already proposed a method, or way, to select an "assessment" (from line 78: "assessment needs to be performed"). Therefore, answer choice A, "A report" is the best answer choice because the European Commission is putting together this information to "report" on their progress.

Madame de Staël Famous Women Series (Pg.40)

1) A - The second and third paragraph serve to establish the relationship between Necker and Geoffrin. The third serves to give status to Madame Necker through her husband's position. The remaining paragraphs are about her childhood.

2) D - The first paragraph establishes the relationship between Necker and Geoffrin by Geoffrin telling an anecdote about a chair. The words "My dear friend" establish their friendship.

3) C - Again, this reinforces their friendship by continuing with "intimacy between them had reached such a pitch" meaning their closeness reached a high point.

4) B - Although Madame Geoffrin and Mister Necker are mentioned in the first four paragraphs of the passage, the purpose is to establish Madame Necker's position

5) B - In the last sentence it states that she reproached herself, expressed disappointment in, or displeasure with her conduct. The conduct being mentioned is in the lines "Mixed with her severe charm there must have been some coquetry, for at a very early age she began making conquests among the young ministers", meaning that she had been flirtatious, coquetry, at an early age with young ministers in order to " to assist Mister Curchod in his duties" or to help her father. Then it says that she was "keeping her numerous admirers simultaneously well in hand", able to deal with people, her father's acquaintances, who liked her.

Car Indoor Air Pollution (Pg.42)

1) C - In lines 32-32 the texts states "Each patrol car was equipped with air quality monitors." This means the study took place inside the cars. The rest of the numbers in paragraph 3 is about the levels of effects the pollution inside the car contained and paragraph 4 is about the illnesses "affects heart-rate variability, thrombosis, and inflammation" (lines 52-53) and the components (mostly elements) "...were calcium, chromium, aldehydes , copper , and sulfur" (lines 69-70).

2) D - This sentence describes 3 things that air quality affects: occupational, environmental medicine, and negative influences on human health.

3) A - The opening sentence states how air quality is important, but the remaining sentences define pollution and anthropomorphic, man-made, pollution, primarily anthropomorphic pollution in lines 6-14.

4) A - Paragraph 3 focuses on nine test subjects, who happen to be Highway Patrol troopers, who are being tested by "air-quality monitors" (in the car) and blood samples to see the effects on of the pollution. The pollution particles had certain negative effects as in lines 37-43 "decreased lymphocytes...." Also, stated again in lines 64-68, "The observations in these healthy young men suggest that in-vehicle exposure to PM2.5 may cause pathophysiologic changes that involve inflammation, coagulation, and cardiac rhythm." The bold being the negative effects. Paragraph 4 continues the negative effects with "exposure to fine PM2.5 from traffic affects heart-rate variability, thrombosis, and inflammation" in lines 53-54. The components of the pollution are stated in

lines 56-58, "The study demonstrated that components that were associated with health endpoints independently from PM2.5 were calcium, chromium, aldehydes, copper, and sulfur."

5) A - The first sentence states, "The changes that were observed in this reanalysis were consistent with effects reported earlier for PM2.5 from speed-change and from soil." which is stating that both studies confirmed the effects for PM2.5. The next sentence continues with "However, the associations of chromium with inflammation markers were not found before for traffic particles." So, this new information found in the second study is updating the report. The paragraph concludes with "elements seem to directly contribute to the inflammatory and cardiac response to PM2.5 from traffic" which is the effects of pollution on the body.

The Spell of the Rockies (Pg.44)

1) B - Every paragraph in the passage describes the fire, conflagration, from the animals, to the narrator.

2) B - The entire paragraph talks about several different animals, herd of elk, Deer, A flock of mountain sheep, coyote, little wolves, of two stealthy mountain lions and each of the animals' reactions to the fire.

3) B - In that sentence, it states all of the destruction, or devastation, that can be seen. Examples are: "a dead forest in a desolate field", "mutilated trees", "a forest ruin", and "impressively picturesque and pathetic."

4) C - Flight means running away, which the animals are doing in the first paragraphs in the entire 1st column. Then the narrator enters himself into the remaining paragraphs, so we can read his personal observations in those paragraphs.

5) D - Morbid means dealing with unpleasant subjects such as death. Phrases such as "the trees just killed were smoking", "the standing dead trees were just beginning to burn freely", "and strangely burned among the multitudinous dead" are morbid because they deal with death while "Weird and strange in the night were the groups of silhouetted figures in a shadow-dance " gives the morbidly creepy feeling of the trees acting like spirits due to the flame's movement.

William James' idea of habit (Pg.46)

1) D - First the text states that animals are "a bundle of habits", then it continues that animals in the wild have a "round of daily behavior... implanted at birth " meaning that they have instincts. The text continues with "in animals domesticated, and especially in man, it seems, to a great extent, to be the result of education" that domesticated animals used by people and humans habits are based on education, or learning. So, it's about "habits based on instinct and education".

2) B - Basically the text in lines 34-36 is saying that evolution and habit help beings to continuously be able to reach perfection since "progressive" means gradually working to and perfectibility means capable of perfection.

3) C - The 2nd paragraph states that "the laws of Nature are nothing but the immutable habits which the different elementary sorts of matter follow in their actions and reactions upon each other." Both lines 22-25 and lines 38-39 are discussing the fact that the laws of nature have to do with habit. However, in the third paragraph line 44, they discuss "adaptive unconscious" which is a theory that "thought and perception" would act "without awareness, and we would remain unconscious", so C contrasts what is being said in paragraph 2 by being mental rather than physical (law of nature).

4) B - Unfold means reveal, or to know the answer to, and automatize means reflexive which in turn means characterized by habitual and unthinking behavior. So, the only correct answer choice is, "Why are organisms' actions reflexive?"

5) D- In the sentence "it diminishes the conscious attention with which our acts are performed." It refers to habit diminishes means lessens conscious effort means focused effort or focused work on acts that are done, or performed. So, all together it means that habit lessens focused work on acts that are done which is D.

Green Infrastructure Opportunities (Pg.48)

1) D - The entire passage is informing the reader of the benefits of implementing green infrastructure. Although line 74 states, "higher installation costs" bringing up a negative aspect, rest of that sentence negates the negativity with, "this is not always the case". The

remaining paragraphs discuss the positive aspects of green infrastructure.

2) A - The opening sentence starts with, "Green infrastructure uses natural processes to improve water quality and manage water quantity," which is stating its purpose, or what it uses. It continues with, "restoring the hydrologic function of the urban landscape, managing stormwater at its source, and reducing the need for additional gray infrastructure in many instances," which states how it will achieve its purpose.

3) D - The first sentence states, "This document provides approaches". This means they want to instruct or show how to do something. "Local government officials and municipal program managers", which are other words for civil servants, "use to incorporate green infrastructure" or to implement green infrastructure. So the answer is D.

4) B - Both "showcase the aesthetic appeal of green infrastructure practices" meaning the beauty of green infrastructure and "provide a visual demonstration of how they can function" meaning building a real, viewable example of green infrastructure explain the benefits of green infrastructure to people.

5) C - The usage of "whereas" lets us know that two things are being compared and contrasted then followed by "green infrastructure" and "gray infrastructure".

Silas Marner (Pg.50)

1) B - Although the beginning of the story illustrates his experience with Eppie in nature, it shifts to how he feels about her mischievous actions, considers the disciplinary actions suggested by Dolly, and the escape of Eppie with scissors, which are all challenges.

2) A - Refuge means to find safety, but in this case, since there is no danger, it can mean relax. So Silas is relaxing in the playfulness of his daughter.

3) C - The first part is obviously Eppie's growth. The second based on these two excerpts "his mind was growing into memory" and "his soul, long stupefied in a cold narrow prison, was unfolding too, and trembling gradually into full consciousness", show his reflection on some past wrong-doings or mistakes since "his soul" is in "a cold narrow prison". He is condemning, or having a feeling of being wrong or evil, himself. So C, one's growth and another's self-condemnation, is the best.

4) D - In paragraph 4 Dolly presents two courses of action for Silas to take to discipline Eppie: smacking, physical punishment, or the coal-hole, locking her up in a dark coal storage space for a short time. So these are two courses of action that are presented to Silas. In paragraph 5 the text

states, "he trembled at a moment's contention with her, lest she should love him the less for it" meaning that he did not want the consequences of contention, or conflict, with her and her not loving him as much. So, the course of action is the smacking and coal-hole, and the consequences are her loving him less for the punishment is choice D.

5) C - Obviously the passage started out with Silas and Eppie, so in fact all 4 answer choices are correct in this respect, but the fourth and fifth paragraphs deal with disciplinary actions for her mischief, or irresponsible playfulness, concluding with the final paragraph being an example of her mischief.

Eisenhower's Farewell Address (Pg.52)

1) D - The first two paragraphs are telling about how the military is necessary. The third is about how it has grown. The fourth is about how the military is felt everywhere. Then Eisenhower begins his warning in the lines 30-33, "In the councils of government, we must guard against the acquisition of unwarranted influence, whether sought or unsought, by the military-industrial complex," meaning we must be careful not to allow the military to influence the government. He continues in the sixth paragraph that such a combination, merger, "endanger our liberties or democratic processes" (lines 36). Paragraphs seven and eight are about technology changing the military. The ninth paragraph is about the Federal govt. controlling scholars. The tenth paragraph is about science and technology leaders controlling the public policy. The eleventh paragraph is about how statesmanship, govt., must maintain a free society. So, everything after the fourth paragraph is a warning of the technologically controlled military would rule over government and the citizens, proving answer choice D correct.

2) B - His basic idea in this statement is that if you have a strong military, then no other military will try to attack you because they could lose or at least lose a lot of their military personnel trying, as the old saying goes "A good offense is the best defense".

3) B - Eisenhower is warning that "the councils of government", the regional governing and/or coordinating bodies that exist throughout the United States, must guard against, "the influence" of the "military-industrial complex" a longer word for the military and all its parts.

4) B - Paragraph 7 states, "and largely responsible for the sweeping changes in our industrial-military posture, has been the technological revolution" which means that the big changes in the military has been the technological revolution, or technological changes. He continues with research (into technology) has been central, very

important, and that research is costly, so the government, pays for it.

In paragraph 8, Eisenhower discusses that the technology is done by a lot of people and organizations which is costly and the government pays for it. So B is the best answer choice.

5) D - Statesmanship means government and Eisenhower is saying that it is the government's task, or job, "to mold, to balance, and to integrate". In other words, manage, "these and other forces", which he means military and its parts (military-industrial complex), and any other powers or components, "within the principles of our democratic system-ever" following the ways of a democratic governmental system, "aiming toward the supreme goals of our free society" to keep our free society.

Short-form mindfulness training in student cohorts (Pg.54)

1) C - The first two words "Mindfulness is…" already tell you that most likely it will be a definition or explanation, then it continues with mindfulness being a mental mode of being in the present without any deep thoughts, conceptual elaboration, or reacting to them, reactivity. The next sentence continues with, "Mindfulness training (MT) programs offer practices", which is telling the reader it offers another explanation. The paragraph ends with what it teaches to do "focus attention on one's present moment" and "mindfulness of breathing".

2) D - The words "the participant is instructed to focus" tells us what the person who is doing Mindfulness training is supposed to do. The rest of the paragraph is about the methods, or methodology, of how the participant follows the practice such as "breathing", "maintain attention on that selected object for the period" and "guide attention back to the target object". All of this is how to do the practice, once again, its methodology.

3) B - In lines 25-26, the text states, "A study compared ....." So, the text is introducing "A study". In line 30 the text states, "The results suggested," which is telling the results of the study. Further down, the paragraph once again brings up the "study" stating, "In addition, since this was a cross-sectional study". So, the central idea of the paragraph is B, a study on Mindfulness training.

4) C - Although the study mentioned in paragraphs four and five are comparing the effects of a study on Mindfulness training and nutrition, the purpose was to learn as in lines 46, "A recent study investigated MT", about how Mindfulness training affects tasks and the

wandering of the mind, which in fact showed that Mindfulness training had better results than just nutrition.

5) D - Again, just as in paragraphs 4 and 5, Mindfulness training affects tasks and the wandering of the mind which is answer choice D.

The La Chance Mine Mystery (Pg.56)

1) C - The beginning of the story is about the hardships of the main character on his journey. Paragraph 7 is about him arriving at a horse refreshing station, or stables and expressing his obligation to get home. Then it concludes in paragraph 8 with him wanting to be in his house. Therefore, C is the closest because it includes going back home.

2) D- Although these 2 paragraphs show how hard his travels were, as in "hardship", "treacherous", and "onerous", the vivid imagery is intended to set up the setting of the story.

3) B - The fact that it was not used for transport tells us that the lake was too dangerous. Throughout history, waterways have always been used for transport, unless they're too dangerous. So, even though it was a lake, it was not like other lakes because of its dangers described later in the paragraph as stated in this excerpt, "It (The lake) would fall in a night to shallows a child could wade through, among bristling needles of rocks no one had ever guessed at; and rise in a morning to the tops of the spruce scrub on its banks,—a sweet spread of water with not a rock to be seen." So basically the water would shallow out, and then rise again making it hard to travel during the shallow times.

4) B - The main point of the paragraph is that there is no fresh horse waiting for the main character to switch off to, so he must stay at this station until a fresh horse come, thus continuing his hardships of not arriving home. Being at home is comfort, being at a "stable" is hardship.

5) D - The main character's journey was obviously suffering, and abeyance means temporary suspension (of his suffering - because we do not know if his suffering will continue after his short rest.)

The Spirit of Youth and the City Streets (Pg.58)

1) A - The opening paragraph states the idea clearly with the keywords "When the work itself offers nothing of interest" meaning it's boring, and "and when no public provision is made for recreation" meaning they have no way to release their stress, and "the situation becomes almost insupportable to the youth" meaning that youth can't stand the situation. Then in the first sentence of the second paragraph, it states, "the joy of youth is well nigh extinguished" meaning joy is nearly, nigh, extinguished,

put out like a fire. The second paragraph continues with, "the young walk almost as wearily and listlessly as the old", meaning that the youth are tired and have no energy. The third paragraph continues with "The modern factory calls for an expenditure of nervous energy" meaning this work causes nervousness, emotional stress and "no one is concerned as to what may be done to aid him in this process and to relieve it of its dullness and difficulty, to mitigate its strain and harshness," further making the point that he has stress. The fourth paragraph continues with "Perhaps never before have young people been expected to work from motives so detached from direct emotional incentive" meaning there is no emotional gain in what the youth are doing. The fifth paragraph continues with "many times results in such nervous irritability that the youth, in spite of all sorts of prudential reasons, "throws up his job," showing that such stress as being nervous makes youth quit their jobs. So, although there are other minor points like youth not having energy, the main point is: Youth do not have emotional outlets.

2) D - In the lines after the given sentence, the author states "the young walk almost as wearily and listlessly as the old" showing that youth are just as tired physically and emotionally as their elders. (That's why you must read at least one sentence before and one sentence after the given sentence to understand the meaning of an author.)

3) C - Lines 17-23 deal with how the youth could express themselves, or portray themselves, through work specifically "people still had a chance to find self-expression in their work". Lines 23-40 are about how the work is restraining or suppressing, stifling, them as seen in "an expenditure of nervous energy ". The lines 26-27, "greater stress is laid upon fine and exact movements necessarily involving nervous strain" and lines 31-32, and lines 32-36 "greater stress is laid upon fine and exact movements necessarily involving nervous strain," also mention this stress. Lines 37-39 ended the line of thought with "The demands made upon his eyes are complicated and trivial, the use of his muscles is fussy and monotonous..."

4) C - The paragraph begins with the negatives of how the youth are being exploited and the exploitation's effects as a build up to the solution which is education.

5) A - The opening sentence of paragraph 6 states, "The revolt of youth against uniformity" meaning the youth who do not follow the others, continues with "throws up his job" meaning quits his job. Paragraph 7 states, "When the boy is on the street, however, and is "standing around on the corner with the gang" meaning he has turned to the street. Paragraph 7 continues with "he finds the difficulties of direct untrammeled action almost as great there as they were in the factory" meaning he experiences life on the street almost as difficult as in the factory. It

then continues with "finds little chance for expression, for he discovers that in whatever really active pursuit he tries to engage, he is promptly suppressed by the police." Whatever he tries to do to express himself on the street, the police stop him finally ending with, "After several futile attempts at self-expression, he returns to his street corner subdued and so far discouraged that when he has the next impulse to vigorous action he concludes that it is of no use" meaning that after trying to express himself a few times and being stopped by the police, he longer has the will to and just finds that his actions have no use.

Citations:

MDPI and ACS Style
Citation: Diaci, J.; Rozenbergar, D.; Fidej, G.; Nagel, T.A. Challenges for Uneven-Aged Silviculture in Restoration of Post-Disturbance Forests in Central Europe: A Synthesis. *Forests* 2017, *8*, 378. (CC BY). (G)

Citation: Blanco CA (2014) The principal sources of William James' idea of habit. *Front. Hum. Neurosci.* 8:274. doi: 10.3389/fnhum.2014.00274 (CC BY). (G)

Citation: Morrison AB, Goolsarran M, Rogers SL and Jha AP (2014) Taming a wandering attention: Short-form mindfulness training in student cohorts. *Front. Hum. Neurosci.* 7:897. doi: 10.3389/fnhum.2013.00897 (CC BY). (G)

Citation: Derbyshire EJ (2017) Flexitarian Diets and Health: A Review of the Evidence-Based Literature. *Front. Nutr.* 3:55. doi: 10.3389/fnut.2016.00055 (CC BY). (G)

Citation: Cochrane SKJ, Andersen JH, Berg T, Blanchet H, Borja A, Carstensen J, Elliott M, Hummel H, Niquil N and Renaud PE (2016) What Is Marine Biodiversity? Towards Common Concepts and Their Implications for Assessing Biodiversity Status. *Front. Mar. Sci.* 3:248. doi: 10.3389/fmars.2016.00248 (CC BY). (G)

Citation: Car indoor air pollution - analysis of potential sources Journal of Occupational Medicine and Toxicology, 2011, Volume 6, Number 1, Page 1 Daniel Müller, Doris Klingelhöfer, Stefanie Uibel, David A Groneberg. (CC BY). (G) The following adaptaions have been made to the original text: From the introduction section only paragraphs 1 & 3 were used. From the particulate matter components section paragraphs 1,2 & 3 were used.

Citation: United States Postal Service. Diary Study Mail Use & Attitudes in FY 2010 The Household Diary Study Mail Use & Attitudes in FY 2010. By John Mazzone - Economist John Pickett - Manager, Revenue and Volume Forecasting Finance and Planning Department. April 2011, Contract #102592-02-B-1502.

Other SAT® Books by Focus on Learning Publishing, LLC.®

Achieving the SAT® Breakthrough: Acing the Types of Questions that Most Students Find Difficult
Focus On: Line Reference Questions

Achieving the SAT® Breakthrough: Acing the Types of Questions that Most Students Find Difficult
Focus on: Vocabulary Questions

Achieving the SAT® Breakthrough: Acing the Types of Questions that Most Students Find Difficult
Focus On: Inference Questions

Achieving the SAT® Breakthrough: Acing the Types of Questions that Most Students Find Difficult
Focus On: Informational Graphics

E-Book – Back to the SAT® Basics: Reading Comprehension for High School Students –
Focus On: Main Idea, Details, and Summarizing with Short News Based Articles

Go to www.folpbooks.com for downloads, books, and updates

Some downloads include:

Free root words and root words' tests
Free SAT® type reading passages to get even more practice with the types of passages on the test
Free extra work on all of our books
And much more!